"You've been using the tool between your ears your whole life, but how often have you considered what it is and what it is good for? No user's manual came with it, but this book helps make up for that shipping mistake. You would not use your dishwasher without cracking the manual. Come on. Time to take a look!"

—Steven C. Hayes, PhD, Foundation Professor of Psychology at the University of Nevada and author of *Get Out of Your Mind and Into Your Life*

The User's Guide
to the
Human Mind

Why Our Brains Make Us
Unhappy, Anxious, *and* Neurotic
and What We Can Do about It

SHAWN T. SMITH, PsyD

New Harbinger Publications, Inc.

Publisher's Note

Distributed in Canada by Raincoast Books

Copyright © 2011 by Shawn T. Smith
New Harbinger Publications, Inc.
5674 Shattuck Avenue
Oakland, CA 94609
www.newharbinger.com

Cover design by Amy Shoup; Text design by Tracy Marie Carlson;
Acquired by Melissa Kirk; Edited by Jean Blomquist

Library of Congress Cataloging-in-Publication Data

Smith, Shawn T., 1967-
  The user's guide to the human mind : why our brains make us unhappy, anxious, and neurotic and what we can do about it / Shawn T. Smith.
    p. cm.
  Includes bibliographical references.
  ISBN 978-1-60882-052-8 (pbk.) -- ISBN 978-1-60882-053-5 (pdf e-book)
  1. Psychology. 2. Emotions. 3. Reason. 4. Brain. I. Title.
  BF121.S59 2011
  152.4--dc23

                    2011027865

13   12   11

10   9   8   7   6   5   4   3   2   1

First printing

For Tracy and Jordan

Contents

Part 1
The Worry Machine

Part 2

Happiness Is Not Your Mind's Job

Part 3

Four Ways Our Minds Coerce Us— and What We Can Do About Them

8

9

10

Part 4

Mood, Lifestyle, and Psychological Flexibility

11

12

Acknowledgments

There would be very few books in print if their authors had to go it alone. This book owes its existence to many people who have stood in my corner. My everlasting gratitude goes to Melissa Kirk at New Harbinger for her faith in me and for shaping this book, and to Jess Beebe, Nicola Skidmore, Kayla Sussel, and Jean Blomquist for their patient and wise editing. To my colleagues who suffered through the early drafts and offered invaluable feedback, I am deeply grateful: Sarah Burgamy, PsyD, Bennett Leslie, PsyD, Jonathan Lipson, PhD, and Christa Smith, PsyD. I also want to thank my many instructors, supervisors, and clients who continue to show me the way. Many thanks to my lovely niece, Valerie Wickwar-Svoboda, for a clear perspective from a master of the English language, and to my friend Penny Oliver for the kind and detailed attention to this manuscript. You both helped me convey what I actually meant to say. Finally, I could not have written this, or accomplished much of anything else, without my family. Thank you Mom, Bob, and Bev for handling some of my responsibilities during this writing, to Jordan for being the bright and shiny center of our little world, and to my wife, Tracy, for your love and endless patience.

Introduction

'm thinking of a vivid memory from childhood. It is one of those flashbulb moments that the mind occasionally casts into our awareness. It happened at closing time at my family's truck stop as I was washing glasses behind the bar. (I had an unusual childhood.) That's when I noticed Chuck, one of our regular customers.

Chuck was one of my favorites. Straw cowboy hat, goose-down vest, and a perpetual grin. He was gregarious, witty, good-natured, and an always-welcomed fixture at the bar.

Chuck also seemed troubled in a way that eluded my ten-year-old mind. He drank heavily, and despite his affability, people knew little about him. He was never at a loss for good conversation, but he rarely discussed himself. He managed to keep the spotlight on others. Someone once joked that he must have been a spy because he was a man of such mystery.

In hindsight, he had the bearing of a man who hoped to avoid an encounter with his own regrets, and so he dodged and weaved using humor, camaraderie, and alcohol. Had you asked me at the time, I might have said that he seemed like a happy guy, but he was probably lonely.

On the evening that I recall, he sat in contrast to his usual manner. He was alone, relaxed, and peaceful. His constant, mischievous grin was replaced by the slightest and most genuine smile. Before him sat a nearly empty glass of beer. It was the last in a chain of empty glasses, and I couldn't decide whether to disturb him so that I could wash it.

Many years have passed since that evening, though I've never forgotten Chuck. I have, however, graduated from junior barkeep's assistant to clinical psychologist. Now I wonder what caused Chuck to drink so much and to avoid revealing who he really was. I wonder what was going through his mind and what his mind was telling him about himself and his life.

I'll never know what Chuck's mind was telling him, but I do know what my mind tells me—and I don't always like it. And if you're anything like me, you may wonder how you can control your mind. If it's like mine, it never shuts up!

In some ways, a mind is easy to control. I can choose to think about what I want, when I want. Right now, I'm choosing to think about donuts, because I like donuts.

In other ways, minds are downright willful and insolent. They think their own thoughts, without permission, and usually with impeccably bad timing. Take my last attempt at public speaking. As I stood in front of a crowd, ready to begin my presentation, my mind gave me these thoughts:

You're going to forget what to say. You need a haircut. Is your fly open?

I didn't want those thoughts. They weren't helpful. Thanks a lot, mind.

Sometimes minds go well beyond these jabs at self-confidence. They can convince us that we are damaged and unlovable, or that we cannot do something within our power, or that the world is more dangerous than it really is. They can saddle us with such powerful anxiety and depression that we believe we cannot do as we wish. Our minds can be that persuasive.

Naturally we try to control and silence our minds so that we can get on with our lives. I may tell myself, *My next speech will be a smashing success, if only I can force my mind to relax and stop thinking.* Sometimes it works. Other times our minds overpower us, and we are forced to find a way around our own thoughts.

Being resourceful creatures, we are usually able to control the mind for brief periods by distracting ourselves. But distraction works only up to a point.

Let's say, for example, that I'll win a million dollars if I can avoid thinking of monkeys. So to keep from thinking of monkeys, I try to distract myself by counting, singing, or skipping rope. It will probably work for a little bit, but deep down I know why I'm engaged in this frantic and pointless activity: to avoid the thought of monkeys. Now I am not merely thinking of monkeys, but imaginary monkeys are making me count, sing, and skip rope. And guess what I'll think of as soon as I stop? Right—monkeys! (See for yourself: try not to think of monkeys and watch what happens.)

We all have "monkeys" that we avoid thinking about. Maybe they are feelings of failure, or fears that we don't belong, or feelings that we're too young, too old, too whatever. Even when we successfully control the mind, thoughts and feelings eventually return. Sometimes they return with such a vengeance that we do everything we can to silence them once again. We may eat, drink, or work too much, or we may find other ways to distract ourselves from our own thoughts and feelings. Doing so perpetuates a painful cycle of avoidance that only strengthens our problem in the long run. Our own minds place us in metaphorical quicksand: the harder we struggle, the worse it gets.

Getting back to Chuck, I sometimes wonder if he was caught in that kind of trap, and whether his peaceful visage after a night of heavy drinking was the look of a person who had found temporary relief from his own mind.

If so, then the peace he found as he sat before an empty glass surely came at a price steeper than a mere hangover. The mind may be silenced for a bit, but it always returns. Silencing the mind in that manner requires constant, exhausting effort.

Fortunately, controlling the mind is not the only option. It is possible to peacefully coexist with our own minds, even to appreciate them and to find the humor in our own inner workings. That task is easier when we peek behind the curtain and expose the mind's motives. When we know what that little bundle of neurons is up to, it's harder for our thoughts to sneak up on us.

This book is meant to offer some guidance toward that end. Be fore-warned, though. I am no guru. I'm just a former junior barkeep who has helped quite a few people come to terms with their own minds. What I offer here is grounded in the work of brilliant behavioral and evolutionary psychologists who precede me, in particular Steven Hayes and other architects of the branch of psychology known as third-wave behaviorism. Let's take a closer look now at what lies ahead.

What This Book Is About

This book is about living with our minds when our minds are driving us crazy. It's about understanding what the mind is doing, why it is doing it, and how we can live our lives anyway. It is about honestly appreciating what our minds give us—even the thoughts and feelings that we do not want—and gently taking the reins when our minds are blocking our way.

In part 1, we'll look at ways in which the mind speaks to us, and how to gain distance from our own thoughts and feelings so we can respond to them with more insight and freedom.

In part 2, we'll discuss how to move forward when the mind wants to protect us from things that we want, but that the mind sees as dangerous.

In part 3, we'll deconstruct some of the underlying mechanisms that keep us mired in unproductive behaviors. When we can observe what's going on behind the scenes, we have the power to make our own choices rather than following the impulses of the mind.

Finally, in part 4, we'll discuss the proper care and feeding of a human mind so that we can reduce the power that it holds over us.

Throughout this book, I refer to the mind as if it were a separate entity. Of course it isn't separate, but if your mind is like my mind, it can certainly seem that way. The brain (the physical structure that gives us a mind—we'll explore the distinction in chapter 2) is built in such a way that most of its functions and drives lie outside our control, just as the bulk of an iceberg lies beneath the water's surface. But just because most of the brain's functions and drives lie outside our control, that doesn't mean that our minds are working against us. To the contrary, their purpose is to keep us safe. I hold two assumptions that will serve as a foundation as we explore the mind's pursuit of safety.

First, different parts of the brain can act on different contingencies. That means that even when we realize we *shouldn't* eat an entire box of cookies, some part of our mind believes it would be useful to do so.

Second, the unwanted thoughts, feelings, memories, and compulsions of our mind exist for a reason, even when we face something as trivial as a cookie. A well-functioning mind knows that salt, sugar, and fat are rare commodities—or at least they were rare in the primitive environment. That's where our brains grew up, and the circuitry that we developed to survive in a younger and more challenging world continues to drive us to this day. *Better eat that cookie while you can,* says a well-oiled, survival-driven mind, *the opportunity may not come again!* Because they constantly "worry" about our survival, I call our minds "worry machines." But they are worry machines with a very important purpose: they are here to help us—whether we like it or not.

They can be annoying, to be sure. They can mislead us and can even cause pain, but their quirky behavior, to borrow from computer programming parlance, is almost always a feature of the software, not a bug in the program. However abnormal your mind may seem to you, it is probably functioning as it should. But I don't want you to take my word for it. Instead, check my words against your own experience.

Throughout this book, I invite you to do exercises and experiments designed to illuminate your mind's surreptitious attempts to continually direct your behavior in ways both subtle and gross. When we can see what the mind is up to, we can then gain the freedom to respond according to our higher values rather than allowing subconscious processes to direct us. Instead of letting our minds drive us crazy, we can learn to harness, and even appreciate, the mind's naturally protective tendencies.

5

So this is the question before us now: can we win the battle against our own minds? Let's peek behind the curtain of these wondrous worry machines and see what we can see.

Part 1

The Worry Machine

If I were your mind, I would be worried sick about you. Not because you are reckless, but because the world is a dangerous place. It always has been.

If I were your mind, I would carry the experience of a thousand generations who have come and gone. They learned many hard lessons about survival. I would use that wisdom to push you toward safety, even though you might not understand my motives.

If I were your mind, I would be at your side every moment of your life, taking copious, indelible notes each time your body or soul was injured. I wouldn't let you forget about those things.

If I were your mind, I would do everything in my power to protect you. I would insist that you heed my warnings.

But if I were *you*, I wouldn't always listen to my mind.

Chapter 1

Protection at a Price

It can't be normal for my mind to think this much.

I hear that sentiment with surprising frequency. Minds almost always have something to say, and it often seems unhelpful. Minds give us self-doubt when we try to excel; they bury us in history when we want to focus on the future; they bombard us with distraction when we try to concentrate.

Are these minds of ours trying to bring us down?

The natural tendency is to fight the mind by arguing against our thoughts and feelings, or by finding ways to avoid them. Sometimes we win the battle; sometimes the battle creates precisely the situation we hope to avert.

That brings us to likeable Luke, a man caught in an ongoing, self-defeating battle against his own mind. He may need a new strategy.

Luke's Struggle

Luke has an idea. He wants to revolutionize the delivery of industrial lubrication to machine bearings. He has always had an aptitude for solving complex problems, and this is where we begin the story of Luke's suffering.

Luke has a tendency to feel inferior to others. He has long felt overshadowed by his younger sister, who already has an Ivy League education, two wonderful children, and a successful bakery. Luke admires her life, in the manner of someone who desires a thing but could never possess it.

He also feels inferior to his gregarious, all-American big brother. By high school, his brother was dating the most popular girls, playing the most prestigious positions in sports, and even schmoozing a few extra points from teachers who succumbed to his charm. His brother is now an attorney with a six-figure income, and Luke sometimes marvels at the tales of his glamorous lifestyle. Dinners with senators and exotic vacations seem worlds apart from Luke's unassuming lifestyle.

Luke's self-doubt began early in life. While exceptionally bright, he performed poorly in school. The classes bored him. He struggled to stay invested in classes that he could easily have mastered, while his attention wandered to more interesting endeavors. Unbeknownst to his teachers, he spent his extracurricular hours exercising his impressive aptitude for mechanics and electronics.

Somehow the adults in his life never noticed his precocious intellect. They weren't present when he built a functioning rocket from scratch, or when he helped a friend create a fancy, multilevel hamster cage out of old bits of wood and glass. Luke never thought of his projects as extraordinary; they simply made him happy and delighted his friends. Nevertheless, with his mediocre grades, Luke learned to question his abilities. "You're simply not cutting it," a teacher once told him. Luke began to believe that the statement encapsulated his existence.

While Luke was beginning to question his worth, his siblings enjoyed a different existence. Luke watched their academic successes accumulate, while he seemed to slip farther behind. As we all do from time to time, Luke silently compared himself and judged himself to be lacking.

He started to find reasons for what he was beginning to perceive as failure. He experienced the thought that he was unintelligent, or that he simply would never fit in. That idea felt frightening to Luke. He loved having friends and didn't like the idea of losing them.

As Luke approached adulthood, he began to enter social situations with the fear of isolation foremost in his mind. He scrutinized himself in social settings, and he found plenty of things he didn't like about himself—a trap that easily ensnares us. Luke began to think of himself as an outcast.

That fear of social isolation led him to behave awkwardly, and others responded to his hesitance with their own discomfort. Luke's mind began to interpret their behavior as rejection. Just as his siblings' academic successes built upon earlier successes, Luke's fear of social isolation was taking on a life of its own.

That's the problem with owning a human mind. In its effort to solve problems, it sometimes creates the very thing that we fear. That's what happened to bright, capable, likeable Luke.

Judging himself to be inferior despite evidence to the contrary may seem irrational, but there is a certain logic to it. If other people, or bad luck, or angry gods had caused his problem, then the problem would be beyond his control. He would never be able to fix it. But if the problem was within himself, then he might be able to eliminate it if he tried hard enough. So says the typical human mind.

To this day, Luke's mind is trying to solve a problem that never really existed. He was once perfectly at ease with other people; now he can barely hold a conversation without his mind, like an overpowering voice from within, urging him not to bungle the interaction and drive others away. His own mind has become a social impediment.

Which brings us back to the topic of industrial lubrication. Luke learned the value of it while repairing automatic pinsetter machines at the local bowling alley, a job that he earned at a young age thanks to his mechanical ingenuity and his shy but personable nature. While repairing the complex machinery, he noticed the challenge of delivering grease to concealed bearings and other moving parts. A simpler delivery system would lower maintenance costs, and he has devised an ingenious solution to the problem.

As intriguing as his solution might be, industrial lubrication makes for awkward conversation on a first date. That's what happened when he invited Chelsea to dinner. It was almost as if his mind were sitting in the chair next to him, *trying* to make him nervous. *Don't screw this up.... She's out of your league.... Remember all those other dates you've botched? You're just not cutting it.*

Luke's self-doubt was so insistent that he could barely think beyond it. He truly valued intimacy, and he wanted to be in a loving relationship. In a desperate attempt to find something—*anything*—to entertain her, Luke noticed himself prattling on about the cost-benefit ratio of differing lubrication methods. This did not enthrall her. The date ended politely but without hope for a second chance.

Chelsea never had the opportunity to discover Luke's true nature. His anxiety had interfered once again. He decided that he would have to work harder to control his mind next time. Perhaps you have experienced a thought like that. I certainly have.

But maybe "working harder" is precisely the problem. Our minds sometimes toss us into emotional quicksand. The more we struggle against them, the worse the problem becomes. The good news is that there is hope for Luke and anyone else who possesses a self-defeating mind.

My Mind, My Bodyguard

Have you ever wondered why humans are more intelligent than we need to be? Basic survival requires only enough food, shelter, and physical intimacy to launch the next generation, yet our minds give us so much more. We don't need movies, trips to the moon, or chocolate-covered peanuts. We *like* these things, but we don't *need* them. So why are we so intelligent?

The answer lies in the survival value of having a big brain. Our minds are tireless worry machines. They do a fabulous job of protecting us. The downside is that they never stop looking for problems, and they can't be turned off.

Possessing a human mind is a two-edged sword. With their overbearing nature and never-ending stream of thoughts, feelings, and impulses, these worry machines frequently help us achieve precisely the opposite of what we desire.

In a sense, we are all like Luke. Our minds seem to possess us with their worry, their calls to action, and their frequently self-defeating motivations. Luke wanted acceptance and companionship; his mind helped him achieve the opposite. Sometimes the mind acts like a magnet with its poles reversed. It attracts what we hope to avoid and repels that which we desire. The nerve!

Despite the frustration that minds can cause, this book begins with the single notion that there is nothing wrong with a mind like Luke's. I believe his mind was doing exactly what it was supposed to do from a standpoint of safety and survival, and I'll bet yours behaves similarly on occasion.

Sometimes it seems as if we are at cross-purposes with our own minds. That certainly seems true for Luke. He had clear goals and values. He wanted to find someone special with whom he could be a loving partner. His mind, on the other hand, was more interested in protecting him from the very real risk of rejection. Luke's goal was romance. His mind's goal was survival.

Throughout this book, I'm going to suggest that your mind is almost always looking out for you, even when it seems to be working against you. You might think of the mind as an overbearing, overprotective sibling. It's the big brother who is forever monitoring and meddling, but it means well.

Admittedly, that's an odd way to look at things. Sometimes it seems to make more sense to believe that there's something broken about our minds. Why else would we overeat, get depressed, worry about the future, ruminate on anger, and avoid exercise? Why else would our minds let us down precisely when we need them the most, as Luke's did? If our minds are really trying to protect us, shouldn't it be easy to do what we want, get what we want, and be who we want to be?

From the mind's point of view, the answer must sometimes be no. The mind must follow certain rules, like putting our safety and survival above all else, avoiding pain, and making sure that our needs are met for the moment.

Where I come from—a culture of hardy Midwesterners who survived the Great Depression and the Great Dust Bowl—the conventional wisdom is to argue against the mind. *Stop feeling sorry for yourself. Pull yourself up by your bootstraps and soldier on.*

There's a good bit of wisdom in that. An impressive array of psychological techniques has been developed to help us argue our minds into submission when they're denying our wishes or supplying too much pain. But arguing with the mind may not always be the most useful choice. Sometimes, accepting the mind—even appreciating it—is more practical.

The Argument Trap

The mind often gives us things that we don't want—thoughts, feelings, memories, anxieties, moods, and even physical sensations like a pounding heart or sweaty armpits. Sometimes it happens out of the blue; other times the mind throws a fit because we have dragged it into a situation it hoped to avoid (like a first date where rejection is a real possibility). When the mind begins to beat up on us, we have a choice: accept what it is giving us or try to change it. We will be talking much more about the acceptance option. For now, let's look at what frequently happens when we argue with our minds.

Consider one of the most common fears among humans: public speaking. Other animals don't possess this fear simply because they don't make speeches. However, if animals did make speeches, it's a safe bet that the ones who gave speeches would experience a similar fear—if they were concerned with the opinions of others.

Fear of public speaking typically follows from the fear of being scrutinized by others. As pack animals, humans are wired to understand that public scrutiny can exact a cost, such as being ostracized by the group. Social acceptance matters to us because we are ill equipped to survive without others.

Dogs, also being pack animals, would probably suffer public-speaking anxiety because placing themselves in the spotlight might affect their standing in the pack. A poorly executed presentation on begging for table scraps could lead the other dogs to question the speaker's competence. That could snowball into ostracism, or at least seriously diminished social opportunities such as mating.

(Cats, being more solitary, could probably deliver a speech with the confidence that arises from a complete disregard for social acceptance.)

Here in the human community, the mind's protestations come in the form of anxiety and fear, which often manifest physically: sweaty palms, racing heart, upset stomach. This is the mind urging us to run and hide.

We have options when the mind urges us to avoid a situation:

1. Do as it says and retreat from the situation. This offers short-term relief but often comes with the long-term cost of shame and regret.

2. Eliminate discomfort by arguing with our minds so that we no longer encounter unwanted thoughts or emotions.

3. Embrace the discomfort that the mind is providing and move forward anyway. This comes with the possibility of strong short-term discomfort, and higher rewards in the long run. Sometimes—not always—the discomfort disappears in the process.

As you may have already guessed, this book focuses on the third option: accept what the mind gives us and move forward anyway. That can be an unattractive prospect at first glance, and you may be experiencing a reaction from within: *Embrace what?! My mind is out of control, and I'm not about to embrace it!* Before you commit to either embracing or eliminating thoughts and feelings, let's examine what happens when we argue with our minds.

Sometimes arguing works, particularly if we follow the formula for identifying and outmaneuvering what some psychologists call *irrational thoughts*—these are thoughts that are compelling and seem true but don't jibe with evidence from the real world.

For example, the irrational thought that usually exists behind the fear of public speaking is an overestimation of the negative consequences that might follow a poorly delivered speech (Nelson et al. 2010). I might mistakenly believe that a bad speech could destroy my career or my friendships, or that I will lose control on stage and hopelessly embarrass myself.

The irrational thoughts that drive us are rarely visible to the naked eye. Instead, they tend to manifest as a vague sense of dread or anxiety. Before giving a speech, I may be quite aware of my sweaty palms or other physical manifestations of anxiety, but mostly unaware of what's happening beneath the surface: I am probably overestimating negative outcomes.

Challenging and disputing the irrational thought involves putting words to that vague sense of dread. *I'm afraid I'll lose my job if I give a bad speech; I'm afraid I'll freak out and embarrass myself.* Once it's out in the open, we can argue with it. In all probability, most people will not lose their career, destroy friendships, freak out, or go bankrupt after giving a bad speech.

This approach sometimes helps (Block and Wulfert 2000). Sometimes, the guiding light of rational thought gives us the strength to follow our values and do as we wish (give a speech), rather than doing what our minds demand of us (*Run away! Hide!*).

Psychology textbooks are brimming with examples of irrational thinking. Consider these, any one of which could be triggered by the stress of public speaking (adapted from Dryden and Ellis 2001):

All-or-none thinking: If I fail at this speech, which I must not do, it will mean that I am unworthy of love or respect.

Catastrophizing: If they see me fail, they will view me as incompetent and I will be fired.

Focusing on the negative: Because it is unacceptable for things to go wrong, and things often go wrong, my life is no good.

Disqualifying the positive: When they compliment my speech, they are only being kind and forgetting all the stupid things I do.

Minimization: If the speech goes well, it's due to luck. If it goes poorly, it's because I'm completely incompetent.

Personalization: If they laugh, it must be because I'm doing so poorly.

Once they are identified and put into words, these irrational thoughts can sometimes be shot down with challenges to their logic. *Where is the evidence that I am unworthy of love? How do I know that they think I'm incompetent? Who says that they're laughing at me?*

If all goes well, the mind backs down as we come to realize that our thoughts don't match reality. It works best when the mind is already relatively calm. But minds are not always so well behaved. An anxious mind does not calmly defer to logic.

An anxious mind doesn't understand that poorly executed speeches are rarely disastrous. Fires are disastrous. Floods are terrible. Airplane crashes are killers. Disapproving jeers from a hostile audience, on the other hand, rarely end in bloodshed or exile. But the mind sees something different. The experience of a thousand generations who preceded us have shaped our brains to be reactive to certain threats. High on the list are things like abandonment. What could be worse for a human than to be left defenseless and alone?

As we will discuss in the next chapter, we are wired for a simpler and more hostile world where small problems had big consequences. For the most part, humans no longer need to worry about starving, freezing, or being eaten by predators, but our minds, which grew up facing life and death decisions on the savanna, may not have received the memo.

From the mind's point of view, there is no "irrational" fear of social judgment. We may think it's outdated and misapplied at times, but it is hardly unreasonable for a mind to fear being judged harshly and possibly ostracized. Fears like that one seem to be wired into us (Hoffman and Moscovitch 2002). That's why arguing doesn't always work. What can we do if we cannot suppress such thoughts and feelings?

The Paradox of Thought Suppression

Sometimes arguing simply makes things worse, which causes us to struggle harder against the mind—which in turn makes things worse still, and so on. The public speaker who scolds himself to calm down may notice that his anxiety only increases, and so he tries even harder to calm himself. Before he knows it, and without his full awareness, he can be drawn into a futile struggle against his own thoughts and feelings.

When our attempts to control the mind fail, we can find ourselves in the risky pursuit of trying to suppress our own thoughts or emotions. Ironically, the attempt to suppress thoughts and feelings can lead to an increase in those thoughts, along with an increase in the problems that they cause (Wegner et al. 1987; Lavy and van den Hout 1990; Rassin 2005).

For example, a person who tries to avoid thoughts of food in the interest of dieting will probably notice an increase in food-related thoughts, along with an increase in overeating (Barnes and Tantleff-Dunn 2010). This is what makes suppression of thoughts and feelings so risky. There can be harmful consequences. Reasoning with the mind is fine when we can persuade it to come along willingly, but suppressing anxiety, depression, or unpleasant thoughts is like telling yourself to not think of a monkey. You may recall how miserably I failed at that task in the introduction.

Anxiety is a good example of the way in which things can backfire when we argue with the mind. Imagine that you're strapped to a machine designed to detect the faintest signs of worry. Now suppose you're told that if you worry, even a little bit, you will receive an electric shock. Your task is simple: don't worry. As you see yourself being strapped into the machine, don't worry. As the electrodes are clamped to your head, don't worry. As you wonder how painful the shock will be, don't worry.

This is how anxiety can spin out of control. Each time you worry and receive a shock, you will become more motivated to avoid worry. Eventually, the mere thought of anxiety will provoke anxiety. It's quite a conundrum (adapted from Hayes, Strosahl, and Wilson 1999).

There are real consequences to thought suppression. It has been implicated in anxiety problems like obsessive-compulsive disorder (Purdon, Rowa, and Antony 2005). The experience of an anxiety disorder can be every bit as painful as electric shock. As people become increasingly motivated to avoid anxiety, the anxiety tends to worsen. Ironically, attempting to avoid anxiety becomes increasingly anxiety provoking. We simply cannot avoid a thought or feeling that we're focused on avoiding—especially when the mind is worried about survival.

The different forms of anxiety are just a few examples of the fallout that can come from the mind trying to do its job. Throughout the book, we'll be discussing problems of the human spirit, ranging from anxiety to depression to compulsive behaviors like substance abuse. All of them have something in common: a mind carrying out its duties, or at the very least operating on lessons handed down through thousands of generations of expert survivors.

For now, let's get back to the question of arguing with the mind. When is it the right thing to do? I believe the answer is fairly straightforward. If arguing with the mind works, then do it. If it makes the situation worse, then stop. (Don't worry, we will discuss what to do instead.)

Had Luke tried reasoning with his mind by identifying his root fear and debunking it, he would have known in fairly short order whether or not arguing would be effective against that fear.

If it were working, he might have felt a small boost in confidence or fewer physical manifestations of anxiety (sweaty palms and the like). At the very least, he might have felt the confidence that comes from knowing he could overcome whatever self-defeating thought his mind gave him. *She's out of your league*, it might say, to which he would answer, *I'm a good guy and I would treat her right.* If that does the trick, then problem solved.

If, on the other hand, Luke's mind truly believes that she is out of his league, and that rejection is intolerable, then it will do everything in its power to help him avoid it.

Cue the anxiety and the vague sense of dread. *She's out of your league,* says his mind. *Stop it, stop it, stop it,* he answers. Now Luke is no longer trying to reason with his mind, he is in a battle for control.

That is a battle he is unlikely to win. In short order, he will notice his anxiety rising and his mind running away with him. That's a good indication that arguing with the mind isn't working.

Like most of us, Luke probably has little experience with a different option: thanking the mind for trying to help, and moving forward without struggling to control thoughts and feelings. Why struggle against something that's guarding your best interests?

Accepting the mind is sometimes the most useful strategy. When the mind believes that safety or survival is at stake, it won't be outmaneuvered. But that doesn't mean we need to suffer. In a tug-of-war against an immovable force, it makes sense to drop the rope. We'll be discussing how to do that.

Before we move on, let's begin studying how your particular mind functions.

Exercise: How Does Your Mind Speak to You?

This exercise has to do with simply understanding how your mind speaks to you, particularly in times of discomfort. You can begin this exercise in a quiet place, and then practice in the real world, in real time, as you become more skilled. If you wish to proceed, I'll simply be asking you to recall an unpleasant situation of your choosing.

To begin, imagine yourself in a situation like Luke's in which your mind may have been protesting. Choose a time when you felt mildly nervous or concerned in a social situation. Please do not pick a time when you were truly in danger.

As you recall yourself in that uncomfortable situation, visualize the surroundings and the people. Recall the interactions and the events. Who's there? What are they saying? How are you responding? Create as vivid a picture for yourself as possible, including sights, sounds, and smells.

As the situation plays out in your mind, take an inventory of your physical, emotional, and mental states.

What do you feel in your body as the tension rises? Are your muscles clenching? Is your heart pounding? Is your posture changing?

What emotions do you feel? Fear? Anger? The desire to run or fight? Do you feel frozen?

Finally, what thoughts do you notice? What would your mind write it if could pin a note to your lapel? Here's an example:

Dear You,

I'm worried that we look silly, and I wish we could magically disappear from this situation.

Sincerely,
Your Mind

Take a few moments to put words to these feelings, sensations, and thoughts. Describe them to yourself, and try to be precise. For example, I'm noticing a tight sensation in my chest, the feeling that I should run away, and the thought that I must look silly. Be descriptive, and feel free to write your observations on a piece of paper or in a journal. The more ways we can put words to the mind's activities, the better.

Don't linger too long on this exercise. A few minutes should suffice. When you're done, take a few deep breaths, take an inventory of your current surroundings, and remind yourself that you are safe. This is an important part of the exercise, because some part of your mind may still be lingering on the unpleasant situation you imagined.

With practice, you should be able to do this kind of noticing in the real world as situations are unfolding. You may begin to notice that labeling the mind's activities somehow diminishes their power. As these thoughts, feelings, and physical sensations show up in your day-to-day life, you may be increasingly able to label them as simply a message from the mind rather than a problem that must be fixed.

As Luke can attest, the mind can intervene at the worst times, and in the worst ways. I have suggested that it is normal for a mind to do so, and that battling against the mind may actually make the problem worse. You might be wondering how it's possible for a troubled mind to be normal, especially when it causes pain or clearly interferes with our goals. In the next chapter, we'll explore why the mind does what it does, and how experiences like depression and anxiety may actually be designed to help us.

Chapter 2

A Day in the Life of a Mind

Sometimes all we want is a moment's peace, but our minds are whizzing along at five hundred thoughts per hour, chattering, repeating themselves, and inventing new worries.

Nothing could be more normal. Eastern philosophies have long recognized the uncontrollable and ever-chattering mind, as have Western thinkers like Descartes, who noticed that the mind seems like a separate entity that exists for the purpose of thinking.

Psychologists have been contemplating the ubiquity of the chattering mind as far back as the 1800s, when William James (1892) wrote about streams of consciousness and constantly changing states of mind.

Our minds simply never stop churning away. Having read that, if your mind is like my mind, it might be saying something like this: *Sure, everyone thinks a lot, but not like me. My brain is out of control. I am definitely abnormal.* If so, thank your mind for its concern about your normalcy. Then let's move on, beginning with a brief detour into the biology behind that endless chattering. Sometimes it helps to know why it is normal to feel abnormal.

What Is the Mind?

Wouldn't it be nice to simply walk away from the mind's chatter? To leave it standing there, in midsentence, aghast at your insolence? Sometimes it feels as if our minds are separate entities following us around and whispering end-less commentary in our ears.

A separate entity, distinct from us in its vantage point, its concerns, and its motives—that's not a bad way to think about the mind. In order to under-stand the nature of the mind, and why it can feel separate from us, it helps to know a bit about how the brain works.

Let's start with the experience of talking to ourselves. Sometimes we choose the topic, sometimes the topic chooses us. Either way, owning a human mind means tolerating a lot of chatter.

As researcher Chris Fields noted (2002), most of us talk to ourselves, silently, most of the time. Where does this voice come from? Why do we use it so much, and why can't we easily silence it? The answer may lie in the modular construction of the brain. Different systems do different jobs, and many of them operate with some autonomy (like the collection of systems that allow us to talk to ourselves) or with full autonomy (such as the systems that regulate heartbeat and digestion).

Fields suggests that the voice you "hear" when you talk to yourself ema-nates from the same auditory system of the brain that allows us to hear the outside world, except that the impulses are generated from the higher centers of the brain rather than from our ears. It's a self-contained form of hearing that involves no real sound.

The same appears to hold true for visual imagination. Closing our eyes and visualizing a scene activates the same visual systems we use to see the outside world (Kosslyn et al. 1995). Sometimes the mind decides to provide us with visual images without our consent. It happens in dreams, flashbacks, and any time the scent of baking apples conjures the image of a pie.

The point is, our brains are made up of specialized systems that process and exchange information. We are aware of some of our brain's activity, while other functions lie beneath our awareness. We might think of these as "con-scious" and "subconscious" activities.

It appears that some of the brain's systems know things that we do not consciously recognize. For example, there is a certain type of visual impairment called "cortical blindness" that illustrates the type of events bustling beneath the veneer of consciousness. When I was training to become a psychologist, I heard the story of a man who suffered complete blindness after a serious blow to the head. Despite his utter lack of vision, he was strangely able to navigate hallways and deftly avoid collisions. When asked how he did this, he replied, "I don't know."

The explanation is that, while his eyes were fine, the visual cortex on the surface of his brain was damaged. But much deeper in his brain, a way station for visual information (the superior colliculus, in case you care) was functioning just fine, passing visual information from his eyes to other areas of the brain that allowed him to dodge and weave.

The modular brain is a busy place. It gives us images without seeing and sounds without hearing. It sorts stunning amounts of information so that we can attend to our environment. It even chews on problems while we attend to other things. Anyone who has experienced an epiphany or spontaneously recalled a lost bit of information knows the beauty of a mind solving problems on autopilot. Much of the mental activity we associate with being human is the product of such activity. Churning away beneath our conscious awareness are physical structures and computational systems that give us abstract experiences like empathy (Hooker et al. 2010) and intuition (Lieberman 2000).

It is difficult to point to a dividing line between our conscious and subconscious minds. To find that line, we might follow the biological explanations offered by researchers who have identified structures that create a sense of self (Lou et al. 2010), along with systems that give us the ability to monitor our own behavior (Kircher and Leube 2003). According to this line of research, certain parts of the brain function specifically to create self-awareness.

Why does any of this matter? The remainder of this book will require us to have a clear definition of the mind—or at least a definition as clear as our understanding of the brain will allow. This thing that chatters at us constantly is not an aberration, nor is it broken. It is a stunning array of systems designed to guide our behavior. It cannot always speak to us in words, but it does find a way to communicate. Experiences like empathy and intuition, for example, may show up as feelings or urges from deep within. As with cortical blindness, sometimes the mind uses such feelings and impulses to control our behavior without our conscious awareness.

Those are just a couple of examples. The mind also speaks to us through unpleasant experiences like anxiety and depression, which we will discuss later in this chapter.

So what is the mind? To echo the sentiments of Steven Pinker (2007), the mind is what the brain does. And it never stops doing it. That endless chatter you hear? Think of it as the hum of a finely tuned engine.

Why the Mind Worries

Stop and smell the roses, goes the old bromide. Trite as it is, we sometimes need that advice. However, it's no surprise that we need no reminders to stop and look for danger. Our minds are wired for it.

These minds of ours are the results of thousands of generations' worth of good decisions. Any human who successfully navigated the early environment long enough to pass on his or her genes also passed on the tendency to make the decisions that helped that person survive. Their decisions helped shape the circuitry that we carry to this day.

In a very real sense, our minds—the combined systems that churn away beneath our conscious awareness—are primitive minds built for a primitive environment. Timid and reactive, they are always looking for the safe bet.

Our ancestors faced serious environmental dangers. Imagine hiking on the savanna, searching for lunch, when you hear the rustling of leaves nearby. It *might* simply be the wind or a bird taking flight, or some other innocuous thing that can safely be ignored. But the safe bet—the bet that gives the greatest chance of survival—is that the rustling leaves indicate the presence of something dangerous.

We still carry that mental wiring. Whether the stimulus is the rustling of leaves on an ancient savanna or any other unexpected noise that startles us, the mind reacts in the same way. It will take the safe bet and assume the presence of something dangerous, jolting us into a state of hyperawareness. We startle, freeze, and look for signs of threat as our minds cause the release of adrenaline. Our vision and hearing sharpen, while our bodies prepare for quick action. Our minds search for signs of danger—signs that we understand on a primitive and visceral level. Even infants, for example, have the ability to distinguish predatory pursuit from other forms of movement in the environment, and humans possess a finely tuned, natural ability to read the intent of predatory animals (Barrett 2005).

This is a big response to a little noise, but the mind is nothing if not pragmatic. If the rustling turns out to be a bird, or a benign stack of papers moved about by a draft, then nothing is lost by responding as if there had been a serious threat. On the other hand, reacting with calmness and relaxed defenses is the sucker's bet: nothing to gain and everything to lose if there is danger lurking.

Environmental threats are only part of what the mind worries about. The more complicated threats lie within our own species, where we must navigate conflicts over status, resources, and mates. All of these had a direct impact on survival and procreation in the ancestral environment.

For our ancestors, there may have been no more complex or ever-present threat than dealing with other people. Pity the poor forager who didn't understand or couldn't respond when his clansmen tested his mettle by poking fun at him. He was destined for the lower rungs of the social ladder, at best. At worst, he might become an outcast with a very bleak future.

Just as our minds have adapted to a dangerous physical environment, they have also adapted to the complexities and dangers of living among humans. We inherently understand how to compare ourselves to others, guard scarce resources, detect deceit and guile, and avoid social situations that hold the potential for violence (Duntley 2005).

These are just a few examples of a mind that is built for survival. We can thank our ancestors for that—the ones who survived long enough to procreate, anyway. We have inherited minds with a certain outlook on life. We can call it *useful paranoia*, the ongoing output of a mind wired to survive in a complex world.

How the Mind Speaks

The way in which the mind speaks about this complex world with its many complex dangers is both subtle and obvious. Sometimes its messages are clear as a bell; other times the mind influences our behavior more obliquely, like a subtle breeze affecting the trajectory of an airplane. Suddenly, you wonder how you got so far off course.

As a young child, I learned about the mind's more aggressive and obvious messages when I encountered an unleashed German shepherd lounging on the grass of a neighbor's house. Being an animal lover, I walked toward him, smiling broadly, and shouted, "Hi, Doggy!"

My hope was to befriend him for life, but he must have perceived a threat from this goofy, bespectacled kid. In an instant, he was chasing me across the street, biting at my legs. Minds tend to remember events that have a great deal of emotion attached to them. For the remainder of my childhood, I avoided unleashed dogs, because I had learned how dangerous they can be.

Minds do not let go of lessons like that. To this day, the sight of any large dog causes my mind to give me vivid flashbulb memories of that event. It doesn't seem to realize that the event took place more than thirty-five years ago. Despite countless positive interactions with dogs since, my mind still gives me the same old message on occasion: *Stay away! Those teeth are sharp!* The truth is, sometimes dogs are dangerous, sometimes they aren't. Many factors are involved. But my mind isn't interested in shades of gray. It's taking the safe bet.

The mind can also communicate indirectly. Consider intuition, for example. Its purpose seems to be to help us accurately read the environment and other people, in order to avoid problems. Perhaps you have experienced something like a gut feeling that the driver in the next lane is about to suddenly veer into your lane. Far from being mystical or magical, intuition may very well be a function of the modular brain engaged in behind-the-scenes problem solving.

Intuition has been tied to *implicit learning*, the process of learning complex information without effort or awareness (Lieberman 2000). Researcher Carol Augart Seger (1994) pointed to specific areas of the brain associated with implicit learning, as well as some specific forms of this type of information processing. The mind seems to be particularly adept at learning and responding to patterns of which we are consciously unaware, meaning that even when we aren't paying attention to the subtleties of our environment, our minds are (Mathews et al. 2000). That may explain the "gut feeling" that another driver is about to swerve into your lane. The mind is probably picking up on subtle cues such as a slight change in speed, a small movement of the other driver's head, or a barely perceptible drift from the other car. Knowledge like that comes about only from experience, and the "feeling" that we experience is the mind's subtle, nonverbal communication.

Sometimes the best response to intuition is to allow the mind to respond for us, as when we automatically veer out of the other driver's way. When the situation is less pressing, it helps to put words to the intuitive experience: *I'm feeling hesitant about this situation. Why might that be?* Often, simply recognizing and verbalizing our internal experiences is enough to add clarity.

Implicit learning and subtle messages are standard fare in the daily life of a mind. Of course, sometimes the mind needs to take a more hands-on approach. When the mind fears for our safety, it grabs our attention much more aggressively.

Anxiety and Depression: Ancient Tools for Modern Times

Sometimes a gentle, intuitive tap on the shoulder simply isn't strong enough, and so the mind grabs us by both lapels and gives us a good, painful shake. But you can bet that even when our minds are beating up on us, they're doing so for a reason. Their methods have served our species well. Up to a point.

Useful Anxiety

Anxiety is one of the mind's blunt instruments. Imagine for a moment that you were doing the job of another person's mind and you needed to get their attention. Maybe you want them to avoid dogs because dogs have been dangerous in the past, or maybe you want them to avoid giving a speech so that others won't judge them harshly. These are the kinds of things minds worry about. They want us to avoid things that seem dangerous.

Here's the hitch: you cannot simply warn them with words. E-mail messages and singing telegrams are not allowed. But you do have access to emotional and physical states. As the person approaches a dog or a stage, you can give them the feeling of fear in order to encourage retreat. You can give them thoughts of tragedy. You can give them heart palpitations, shortness of breath, and stomach cramps. You can immobilize them with debilitating panic.

Just as importantly, you can reward the person by removing these punishing experiences when they comply. You carry the big stick of anxiety. You can hit them with it when they approach the things you want them to avoid, and you can stop hitting them when they conform to your wishes. Simple and effective!

Not everything is a life-and-death matter to be avoided at all costs, and the mind seems to understand this. Anxiety serves a purpose other than simple avoidance. At reasonable levels—not too much and not too little—it can actually improve performance (Yerkes and Dodson 1908).

Perhaps one of the best places to assess the effects of anxiety on performance is in a statistics class. Most people enter their statistics class with some trepidation, and so Jared Keeley and his research team (2008) decided to investigate the effect of anxiety on test scores. He noted that high anxiety and low anxiety corresponded with poor performance, and a midrange, optimal level of anxiety corresponded with the best test scores.

Our ancestors did not face statistics exams, but they did face the need for athletic performance. Their survival sometimes depended on athletic abilities like hunting, hurling spears, or running fast to escape. In an examination of sports performance, John Raglin and Paul Turner (1993) found results similar to the statistics study: the best physical performances were associated with a moderate level of anxiety. Too much or too little anxiety is detrimental to performance.

We typically pay a much lower price for poor performance than our ancestors did. The tradeoff is that we live long enough to experience ongoing anxiety disorders that they probably did not. But even anxiety that rises to the level of a disorder—that is, it prevents the sufferer from living a normal life—may have roots in healthy adaptations to the primitive environment. *Obsessive-compulsive disorder* (OCD) is a troubling affliction characterized by persistent distressing thoughts, usually accompanied by the irresistible drive to repeat unwanted actions such as checking locks or washing hands. There is good evidence that this condition stems from the uniquely human ability to imagine future problems and focus on solving them (Brüne 2006). This is a handy little survival skill, to say the least. A lion with a full belly doesn't hunt, but a human with a full belly gathers food for leaner times in the future. In the modern world, the mind's obsession with whether or not we locked the door is its attempt to save us from the aftermath of not having locked it.

The mind's preoccupation with our safety is also evident in *post-traumatic stress disorder* (PTSD), in which a person suffers persistent reexperiencing of a traumatic event, along with symptoms of extreme anxiety. While the condition is classified as a disorder, I think the more useful view of PTSD is as a set of adaptations carried out in the extreme. Hypervigilence, one of the markers of PTSD, makes sense from the mind's point of view. Why wouldn't it be on the lookout after something terrible happens? Other symptoms, like withdrawal, avoidance, and flashbacks, can similarly be understood as the behaviors of a mind trying to protect us by emphasizing dangers so we will carefully avoid them (Cantor 2005).

Much of what the mind does to cause us pain can be understood as healthy adaptations. The problem is that the mind often tries to save our lives even when our lives aren't really at stake.

Helpful Depression

One needn't stretch the imagination too far to understand how anxiety can further our survival, but what about depression? How could a condition that leaves us feeling worthless, hopeless, and sometimes even suicidal possibly be useful?

Recent research suggests that depression may be another of the mind's adaptive behaviors. Andrews and Thomson (2009) suggest that *rumination* (one of the primary symptoms of depression, in which the mind fixates on unpleasant thoughts) is the mind's way of solving complex problems that require slow, constant processing.

People suffering from depression tend to dwell on problems that do not have clear solutions, such as how to handle a troubled relationship or career difficulties. Andrews and Thomson suggest that this is not an illness; it's an adaptation. Depression hijacks the mind's resources and ensures sustained attention to a problem. This may explain why talk therapy often helps with depression. Therapy helps us isolate and explore different facets of troubling situations, which, according to Andrews and Thomson, is precisely what the mind is trying to accomplish with depressive rumination.

In moderate doses, depression even seems to sharpen some aspects of thinking. Forgas, Goldenberg, and Unkelbach (2009) have demonstrated that low mood is sometimes accompanied by improved memory. People of low mood also tend to process information more effectively, such as an improved ability to concretely and persuasively express ideas (Forgas 2007). Depression helps ensure that we aren't distracted from whatever problem may be threatening our existence—from the mind's point of view, at least.

The Mind Is Always Rational, from a Certain Point of View

In moderate amounts, anxiety and depression can improve our focus and performance. That doesn't mean that depression and anxiety are always useful. In large doses, they are debilitating.

The mind, however, is unrestrained in protecting us. Where our safety is concerned, it tends to take the "hit it with a bigger rock" approach. Useful planning for the future can devolve into OCD, hard lessons learned about the environment can turn into debilitating PTSD, and useful rumination can turn into self-loathing and depression.

· This is perhaps because our primitive minds are fish out of water in the modern world. Our ancestors were consumed with practical concerns like hunting for the next couple of meals. We, on the other hand, have the luxury of many smaller concerns, such as whether or not we locked the front door. The mind, wired for a more primitive time, sometimes relies on blunt methods to protect us in our more refined environment. As Luke discovered, an overreactive, overprotective mind can achieve precisely the opposite of our intentions. They've worked that way since the Paleolithic era, and they aren't about to stop now.

Still, the mind is almost always rational, from a certain point of view. One of the difficulties of owning a human mind is understanding what it's trying to accomplish when it gives us thoughts, emotions, and physical sensations. Part of the challenge before us is to understand what the mind is saying *while* it is speaking to us rather than after the situation has passed. When we understand what it wants, we are free to comply or to choose another course. One of the most unnatural truths about our minds is this: we don't always have to obey them.

Chapter 3

Letting the Mind Do Its Job

The problem with human minds is that they're always trying to save our lives. There are times when they make no distinction between being chased by a bear and being stuck in an elevator.

This is a troubling thing. Our higher, rational selves notice the discrepancy between thoughts and feelings (*I feel like I'm being chased by a bear!*) and what's really happening (*I'm stuck in an elevator, perfectly safe, no bears in sight*). Noticing the mind's misperceptions can make us feel crazy. The natural response is to try to prevent the mind from behaving so irrationally.

This is where we enter double-whammy territory: beating up on ourselves for internal experiences we never requested and do not want. First we get hit with an unwanted, involuntary thought or feeling, and then we beat up on ourselves for experiencing it: *I shouldn't overreact. I shouldn't be depressed. I'm too sad, too nervous, too upset.*

This is a uniquely human trap. It's easy enough to avoid unwanted situations in the world around us. If we fear airplanes, we can take the train. Problem solved. But trying to avoid our internal experience is like trying to avoid our own heartbeat. We cannot escape it, no matter how hard we try.

A panic attack, for example, is not only emotionally painful and physically uncomfortable, but most people find it embarrassing and shameful. Judging oneself as weak for experiencing panic is understandable but only adds to the likelihood of another attack.

The same holds true for depression and sadness. I have lost count of the clients who think their depression is a shameful malfunction of their brain, when it later turned out to be a normal and adaptive reaction to a difficult situation. Judging their minds to be abnormal only added to their reasons for feeling depressed. Double whammy.

We routinely condemn the behavior of our minds as pathological—so much so that we have devised a variety of pills to help us in our battle against the mind. That's not meant to be an indictment of properly prescribed medications, but simply to illustrate the lengths to which we may go to relieve suffering by suppressing or controlling the normal activities of the mind.

And let us not forget the less admired means of managing internal experiences, such as drinking, shopping, eating, gambling, and sexual compulsion. Behaviors like these can consume us when they are an attempt to manage thoughts, feelings, memories, and worries. They work for a little while, and we get to escape our own internal experiences for a short time. However, we pay a high price later as the thoughts and feelings we hoped to escape return stronger than before.

Therein lies the awful quandary of trying to control a mind. The more we try to avoid a thought or feeling, the more present it becomes. (Remember the "don't think of a monkey" experiment?) The person who drinks to avoid experiencing the pain of losing a loved one may get a temporary reprieve, but the memories and feelings will return with a vengeance, compounded by the fallout of alcohol consumption. That, in turn, leads to an even greater desire to escape. Patterns like this can spin out of control.

Yet we often respond to troubling thoughts and feelings by trying to avoid the mind or argue it into submission. Sometimes that works, but sometimes it backfires. Arguing with the mind can prompt it to argue back. Think back to the last time you tried to rescue someone from a self-critical thoughts. Perhaps they graciously acknowledged your message. More likely, they argued with you, offering several points in defense of their self-denigrating thoughts.

A similar process unfolds when we try to suppress our own minds. We get more of what we don't want, often in the form of evidence that the thought is true: *my life is a shambles* because *I can't find a job, and* because *I don't have enough friends, and* because *I can't afford a decent place to live.*

It's one thing to remind ourselves that there are two sides to every story. That can be useful. It's another thing entirely to become caught up in trying to prove the mind wrong. That's usually a losing proposition, because the mind can always come up with one more contrived way to prove its point.

From the Mind's Point of View, Survival Matters Most

We don't have to argue with or avoid our own thoughts. There is another option. For starters, we can recognize that our minds are simply doing what they are designed to do, and that may not be such a bad thing.

Imagine a game show where the object is to answer questions as a mind would—a primitive, protective, emotional mind. Your job is to pretend you are a mind and answer as if you're trying to advance the survival of your owner. The show is called *If I Were Your Mind.* Cue the perky theme music!

As you're called up on stage, the host gives you the first question. You, Mr. or Mrs. Mind, are accompanying your owner on a job interview. He has been unemployed for some time now and needs income. Do you

A. Approach the situation calmly and rationally, rehearsing effective interview strategies?

B. Relax and enjoy the lovely magazines and potted plants in the waiting room with the calm knowledge that he will survive whether or not he wins the job, so he might as well enjoy the moment?

C. Focus like a laser on your owner's insecurities in the service of avoiding failure, rehearse all of the reasons his life will fall apart if he doesn't get this job (so he'll be motivated to not screw it up), inventory the reasons that the interviewer might find him unacceptable, both as an applicant and as a human being (so he'll be motivated to mind his presentation), recall failed interviews, focusing on what went wrong (so he will be motivated to avoid those same mistakes)?

If you guessed C, you win. If I were a mind, I would do everything in my power to prod my owner toward success—or more accurately, to help him avoid failure. I would think about the future and what might happen if he fails. I would think about the past and his costliest mistakes. I would give him anxiety—as if a bear were chasing him—in order to improve his performance. Never mind that bear-evading skills are useless in most job interviews. As a mind, subtlety isn't my strong suit.

Let's try another one. You, Mr. or Mrs. Mind, are accompanying your owner to a board meeting where she will give a presentation. Do you

A. Help her plan her shopping list, since there's nothing to worry about in the near future?

B. Provide her with confident thoughts—her presentation is perfectly prepared and will forever improve the course of her company?

C. Convince her that her career will be devastated if she fails; remind her of the budget-cut rumors and speculate about reasons that her job might be cut if she doesn't perform well; remind her that several of her friends are in the room and they will undoubtedly think less of her if she botches this; and make her feel as if a bear is chasing her because the adrenaline might come in handy?

If you guessed C, come back tomorrow for the bonus round!

Thoughts Are Not Facts

All of this mental torment is in the service of promoting survival. If the mind is only trying to help, then perhaps empathy toward the mind is more useful than antipathy. The mind will not be stopped in its never-ending quest to protect us, so why not approach it with gratitude and detachment?

The first step toward feeling gratitude for your mind's overbearing behavior is to simply notice what it's doing, as it's doing it. This is not nearly as easy as it might sound. If the mind were actually a separate entity that followed us through our lives, we could soon enough learn to simply ignore it. Anyone who followed us around offering a running commentary could be written off as a crackpot, but we can't so easily write off our own minds. If my mind is a crackpot, does that make me a crackpot?

I hope to have convinced you by now that your mind is probably fine. It's just operating under a rather primitive set of assumptions. Now let's see if we can learn how to recognize the mind's motivations.

One of the most fascinating human features is our ability to watch our own minds, which is a bit like being in two places at once. Imagine driving around a racetrack while simultaneously watching our racecar from the stands. We can't do things like that in real life, but we are capable of experiencing thoughts and feelings while simultaneously watching ourselves experience those events.

It takes practice. It's difficult to consistently observe the mind with clarity and objectivity. We become consumed by driving the car, keeping our eyes on the fast-approaching curves. Daily life demands attention, after all. It demands that we sit in the driver's seat. When we are no longer watching the mind, thoughts and emotions can overtake us because we lose sight of the fact that they are just that—thoughts and emotions. But when we recognize these experiences for what they are, we then get to choose whether or not we obey our mind.

A second difficulty in stepping away from the mind is that certain thoughts *feel* entirely factual. That's especially true when compelling emotions like fear or sadness augment our thoughts: *I believe I'm going to fail, and it must be true because I feel anxious.*

Emotions are compelling because they're difficult to shut down. They operate mostly outside of our control, and we should thank our lucky stars for that. A dispassionate mind would make a poor guardian: *There seems to be a lion running toward you. I don't know, maybe you should feel afraid and try to escape. But only if you really think it's necessary—I'm ambivalent on the matter.* It doesn't work that way. Emotions insist that we obey.

But thoughts are not facts, despite the appearance or the feeling of them. Even when a thought is accurate, that does not make it a fact. It is still just a thought. That idea is so important to good mental health that it deserves its own paragraph:

Thoughts are not facts.

At best, our thoughts are reasonably accurate representations of the world. Often, they are misleading and inaccurate. People can become convinced that they are being followed, that the world is flat, or that they left the oven on after they turned it off. The thought doesn't make it true. Even when thoughts are accompanied by strong emotions, which can strengthen the illusion of credibility, the thought remains merely a thought. This also deserves its own paragraph:

Emotions do not turn thoughts into facts.

We can even take this idea in a slightly esoteric direction: there is no such thing as a thought. It is not an object, any more than a heartbeat or a head-scratch is an object. Thinking, beating, and scratching are transient activities. Sometimes they function in a way that serves us; sometimes they don't. Either way, there is a new thought, a new heartbeat, and a new head-scratch right around the corner. None of them are facts. They are activities.

At first, you may find this an uncomfortable way to think about the mind. Most of us have rightly learned to trust our own minds, and so it follows that our thoughts and feelings must be trustworthy. That logic is a bit faulty. It's similar to thinking, *I can't recall my car breaking down, therefore my car will never break down.*

Despite the initial oddness of it, there is value in the realization that thoughts are not facts. This little morsel of insight, which will make more sense after some diligent practice, can free us from a mind's demanding nature. As always, I don't want you to take my word for it. Test it out for yourself. Here's a good experiment.

Exercise: How Factual Is This Thought?

Pick a thought that seems somewhat factual to you. Self-referential thoughts work well, such as **I'm not very good at my job** or **I'm an outstanding lover**. Rate the thought on a scale of 1 to 10, based on how factual the thought seems. A score of 1 means that the thought seems absolutely false, and 10 means it seems absolutely true. Write down the thought and its rating, and put it in your pocket.

Rate the thought again tomorrow, and periodically across several days. Pay particular attention to the thought after you experience incidents related to it. For example, rate a thought such as **I'm not very good at my job** after an interaction with your boss or a coworker.

You will probably notice that the thought seems more factual at one moment and less factual at another.

With practice, it becomes apparent that the feeling of factualness is not necessarily trustworthy.

On one hand, no matter how insistent and persuasively our minds act, they are simply not very reliable when it comes to certain kinds of perception, especially perceptions concerning the self. If you want to gather more reliable evidence about, for example, your effectiveness in the workplace or the bedroom, it's often better to rely on feedback from others rather than on the "facts" that your own mind generates.

On the other hand, sometimes the mind happens to be correct, as with the experience-based intuition that we discussed in chapter 2. So, how do we know whether or not to trust the mind? The first step, I believe, is to prevent the mind from sneaking up on us, to watch it as it goes about the business of minding our survival. How do we uncover the mind's motives? We begin by observing our thoughts.

Observing Your Thoughts

In the movie *A Beautiful Mind*, mathematician John Nash suffers terribly from hallucinations and delusions. More accurately, it's his reaction to those hallucinations that causes his suffering. He assumes that the hallucinations are factual and that they must be acted upon.

Relief comes only when he learns to observe and recognize his mind's activity. He stops fighting the hallucinations and accepts them for what they are: experiences of the mind. In the movie, he learns to live with them. We know this to be an effective strategy in real life for managing hallucinations as well as for more common concerns such as anxiety and depression (Bach et al. 2006; Orsillo et al. 2004; Tai and Turkington 2009).

When we can observe and accept what our mind has to offer, we are freed from the battle of trying to control or eliminate our thoughts and feelings. Remember the monkeys? They're not easily contained.

Observing thought is rather like praying or meditating, in that it can be complex and esoteric or as simple as you wish it to be. For our purposes, it really needn't be complicated. It isn't rocket science, after all. We all have the ability to watch our thoughts and feelings go by. The following simple exercises are designed to improve your mind-watching abilities.

Exercise: Tiny Soldiers on Parade

For this exercise, begin by getting comfortable in a quiet space and closing your eyes. With practice, you will probably be able to do this exercise during your daily activities.

Once you are comfortable, visualize a parade of tiny soldiers marching in front of you. Each soldier is carrying a sign, and each sign has one of your thoughts written on it. Each new thought goes on a sign in this never-ending parade of tiny soldiers. The signs can carry words, images, even sounds and voices. Whatever your mind produces can go on a sign.

If you prefer, your thoughts can float by on leaves flowing in a stream, as clouds in the sky, as credits on a movie screen, or as widgets on a conveyer belt. What matters is that you imagine watching your mind's activities from a distance as the thought parade goes by.

When you notice that you've forgotten what you're doing and you become attached to a particular thought, simply climb back into the bleachers and let the parade resume (adapted from Hayes, Strosahl, and Wilson 1999).

That's the easy part. The hard part is in simply observing your thoughts without trying to change them or make them go away. It may help to remind yourself that none of the thoughts are facts, even if they seem compelling or if it seems that you must do something with them (like make the parade go faster so a particular thought will disappear).

You may also notice that you're experiencing judgments about the thoughts. **I shouldn't be thinking that** or **Only a crazy person would have that thought.** Take those thoughts, put them on a sign, and add them to the parade. They are not facts, and you need not respond to them.

Exercises like this are most useful when practiced regularly. If you like, you can treat it as meditation. If you're like me, and meditation feels like self-inflicted torture, then treat it as a brief visualization requiring no preparation or debriefing. Either way, there's wisdom in an old joke: You know how to get to Carnegie Hall, don't you? Practice, practice, practice.

Observing Your Emotions

Back in the 1960s, Paul MacLean, a physician and researcher, noticed that the human brain consists roughly of three layers. The outer layer, the *cortex*, gives us our higher reasoning abilities. Middle structures are responsible for certain types of learning, emotion, and many other functions. And then there are deep structures responsible for anatomical functions and basic urges.

Dr. MacLean believed at the time that we could reasonably view the brain in the same way we might view an archeological dig site. Newer structures that give us uniquely human behavior and qualities lie near the surface, while older, more primitive structures—the same types of structures one would find in a reptile's brain—are buried deep within (MacLean 1973).

After fifty years of research, it's clear that Dr. MacLean's original theory was simplistic but generally correct in spirit. We do experience drives and emotions similar to other animals, and some of our most primitive and powerful drives fall under the purview of structures deep within the brain. Even the simple mind of a lizard understands the four Fs of life: feeding, fleeing, fighting, and, er...mating. The more basic the emotion, the less control we have over it. We don't have an off switch for emotions like fear.

Emotions also tend to come with strong physical symptoms. Racing hearts, restless bladders, hair standing on end, the intangible quality of exhilaration—we have no more control over these experiences than the emotions that spawn them. Like anything beyond our control, emotions can be pretty darned frustrating. But just like thoughts, emotions need not rule us.

Learning to observe the deep structures of our so-called *reptilian brain* (an overly simplistic term, but it serves our purposes) has benefits similar to observing the mind. It keeps the lizard from sneaking up on us.

Psychologist Marsha Linehan is an expert in dealing with what she more eloquently calls "emotion mind." Dr. Linehan (1993) suggests that one of the most important things a person can do to avoid being overcome by emotion mind is to describe emotional responses in words. Like thoughts, emotions can feel like factual, literal interpretations of the world, according to Dr. Linehan. Putting words to them helps to create distance from emotions. It helps us see them for what they are.

For example, someone experiencing fear before an exam might say to herself, "I'm noticing that my mouth is dry and my heart is beating fast." Doing so is a useful alternative to accepting the mind's fear (*I'm going to fail my test, get kicked out of school, and lose all my friends*) as an accurate reflection of the world. In truth, she may fail her exam, but her life will not come to an end in the way that minds tend to predict (adapted from Linehan, 1993, 64).

As with thoughts, the tricky part about observing emotions is accepting them as they are. There is little point in trying to change them or drive them away. It may help to remind yourself in the midst of an unpleasant emotion that it will pass. No emotion lasts forever.

Observing emotions is slightly different from observing thoughts, since emotional states sometimes have a slippery or vague quality. This next exercise offers some techniques for identifying the motives that underlie our emotions.

Exercise: The Proper Care and Feeding of a Reptilian Brain

Since emotions have a way of sneaking under the radar and driving our behavior without our awareness, we can bring them into the light by asking ourselves about our emotional states, especially during difficult times: What is my emotional, reptilian brain giving me? Is it fear? Anxiety? Anger? Satisfaction? You might also rate the intensity of the feeling on a scale of 1 to 10, with 1 being barely noticeable and 10 being the most intense emotion that you can imagine.

Once you've identified the emotion and its intensity, see if you can identify what it is in response to, and what your reptilian brain would like you to do about it. Fear and anxiety may be telling you to run away from something that, logically, you know to be safe. Elation and craving may be telling you to go toward something that may not be safe.

Whatever the case, it's good to put words to emotions. It's even better to write them down. Talk to your reptilian brain: **Thanks for looking out for me. You go ahead and be afraid if you must; I'll take care of things from here.**

If you watch the emotional messages that come from your mind long enough, you will probably begin to notice trends. Maybe a certain person evokes anxiety, to which you feel compelled to respond with hostility. Or maybe certain situations, like speaking at staff meetings, compel you to try to escape. Or maybe you're simply vulnerable to anger or low mood under certain conditions (we'll discuss that in chapter 12). When the patterns become clear, it will be more difficult for your mind to sneak up on you with emotional urges. You'll see them coming, notice them for what they are, and choose your own deliberate response. Reptilian brains are useful, but they rarely belong in the driver's seat.

Stepping Away from the Reptilian Brain

Sometimes the mind traps us in our emotions. We focus on them without realizing it. It happens when paralyzing fear is all we can think about, or when we are so anxious in a social situation that our overriding desire is to escape in order to stop the anxiety. When that happens, it's time to shift focus.

The alternative to looking inward is to look outward. You can direct your attention away from internal experience by focusing on outside stimuli, such as sounds, the colors in the room, the feel of an object in your hand, or anything else that lies outside the skin. When you recognize that you need a break from the mind's emotions, focus on the five senses.

It's important to approach that type of redirection with compassion for your mind, its emotions, and its thoughts. Redirecting your attention should not be done in the service of stopping thoughts and feelings. We know that can lead to a paradoxical increase in whatever we're trying to suppress. Instead, turn attention outward while allowing your internal events to unfold. Let your thoughts and feelings become the noise in the background while you focus on other things.

The mind is an insistent thing. It seizes our attention by attaching emotion and even physical sensations to our thoughts. If you tried the Tiny Soldiers exercise, you probably noticed how difficult it is to maintain distance from thoughts. Whenever a particularly compelling thought comes along, it tends to seduce us and draw our attention away from the exercise. Before we know it, we've forgotten what we were doing.

Observing the mind is especially difficult when the mind attaches anxiety, fear, joy, or any other strong emotion to a thought. It's during those moments that the mind tries to demand our obedience. I'd like to offer one final exercise before going forward.

Exercise: I Am Experiencing the Thought...

The task is simply to begin using this phrase: "I'm experiencing the thought..."

Whenever you notice a thought or a compelling feeling, put words to it and then attach the phrase "I'm experiencing the thought..." If you're riding the bus and you notice a negative reaction to another person, you might say to yourself, "I'm experiencing the thought that I don't like that person." If you're enjoying a particularly good meal, use the words, "I'm experiencing the thought that this meal is delicious" (adapted from Hayes, Strosahl, and Wilson 1999).

This exercise is a simple and powerful way to gain distance from the mind's messages. The more you practice, the better. Since it's such an easy exercise to forget, you might place reminders where you will periodically see them.

In upcoming chapters, we will discuss some of the particular mental traits that make humans vulnerable to depression, anxiety, addiction, and other problems in living. But before going forward, I recommend that you spend a few days practicing the exercises in this chapter so you'll be better able to see what your mind is doing from a distance. As the old bumper-sticker adage goes, "Don't believe everything you think."

Part 2

Happiness Is Not Your Mind's Job

One morning a rancher set out to repair a section of fence through which his cattle had been escaping. He rounded up the animals, herded them to a safe corner of the pasture, then rode back to begin work on the fence. As soon as he arrived, he noticed a problem in the distance. The cattle were beginning to wander, and some of them were slowly headed toward the damaged section of fence.

Again, he mounted up and herded the cattle to a safe corner of the pasture. He returned to the fence only to notice that the cattle were, once again, wandering in all directions. Each time he would drive them back into the corner.

When he arrived home at sunset, his wife asked if he had repaired the fence.

"No," said the rancher. "I never got around to mending the fence because those cattle just wouldn't stay in one spot."

Our own minds can put us in a similar predicament when we believe that we cannot move forward until our thoughts and emotions are in order. We tend to feel stuck until our minds are under control. We believe we cannot give a speech until we feel relaxed, go on a date until we feel happy, or change careers until we feel confident.

With our unruly, overprotective minds, we can spend a lifetime waiting until we feel that we are ready to act—unless we find another option.

Chapter 4

How the Mind Uses History

There's no doubt about it, the mind is a voracious, history-gathering machine. That makes us phenomenal learners, which also comes at a price. The mind naturally wants to prevent us from repeating painful experiences. Sometimes it gets carried away, placing undue limitations on our behavior. In this chapter, we'll look at a different way to relate to our own history when the past exerts too much control over our lives, which is exactly what happened to Penelope.

How Penelope Lost Track of Her Values

Somewhere along the way, Penelope lost what is most important to her.

Penelope prides herself on boldness and nonconformity. As a child, she was known to wear different colored socks and eat marshmallow sandwiches for lunch. As an adult, she is just as distinctive. While her friends pursued traditional careers like accounting and dentistry, Penelope studied magic and ultimately found a respectable following as an entertainer.

Hers is a career with plenty of pressures and great rewards. Even though each minutely choreographed show must unfold with perfect timing, she doesn't mind the pressure or the stage fright. Each performance comes with rewards. She especially loves applause because it means that she has brought joy to others.

Rising in the morning and bringing joy to others is the meaning of life, as she sees it. She is a woman of strong convictions, which makes the events of two years ago all the more painful for her.

It was a small thing at first. As she sat at a stoplight one morning, her car was rear-ended. No one was hurt, but the accident was frightening enough that she had difficulty concentrating at work that evening and accidentally exposed the secret to one of her illusions. The audience applauded that night, but with slightly less enthusiasm than she was accustomed to. This troubled her.

The next time she drove through that intersection on the way to a show, an odd thing happened. Her mind started protecting her, as minds will do. *Be careful! Don't get rear-ended! Hey, remember how you bungled that magic trick? Don't do that again!* To punctuate the point, her mind even gave her an anxious rush of adrenaline and the feeling of tightness in her chest. As she sat at that red light for what felt like an eternity, she found herself checking her rearview mirror and fretting that she would make mistakes in her performance.

Not wanting to experience those thoughts and feelings again, and being a quick learner, Penelope began avoiding that particular intersection. She took the long way around, even though it increased her drive time. She didn't like that one bit, but it was better than the memories and anxious sensations her mind gave her when she drove through that intersection.

She thought she had solved the problem: if she could simply avoid that intersection, she wouldn't have to experience the anxiety. But there was a flaw in her strategy. In the back of her mind, she knew that she was avoiding the intersection in order to avoid the thoughts and feelings that her mind had associated with it. A chain of events was developing. Whenever she thought about avoiding the intersection, the same thoughts, feelings, and anxiety began to creep in as if she were actually driving through the intersection. Soon enough, the thought of avoiding the intersection was nearly as anxiety provoking as the intersection itself.

So she did the next logical thing. She began limiting her driving and scheduling fewer performances. The act of getting into her car was enough to bring on the butterflies, the adrenaline, and the terribly embarrassing memory of botching a magic trick in front of dozens of paying customers. By staying home, she was able to avoid that experience.

Unfortunately, logic had once again misled her. In the back of her mind, she knew that she was avoiding her car in order to avoid the unpleasant thoughts and feelings, and that somehow made the anxiety even more present. She began to sense that the anxiety was making her world smaller.

And so, once again, she did the thing that seemed most logical: she began holing up in her house to avoid the thought of going outside, which her mind had come to associate with…well, you know the rest.

That's when a new form of pain set in for Penelope. She noticed that she was not doing the things that were most important to her. She was not getting out of bed every day with the intent of bringing joy to others. Instead, her life had come to be defined by fear. Her world had become small and safe. She began to feel deeply ashamed.

While she was acutely aware of the embarrassment she felt over the anxiety that had taken over her life—it felt like an ugly weed that had overrun her beautiful garden—there were other processes happening in her mind of which she less aware.

She was not very aware, for example, that every show, every smile from a fan, and every minor interaction she had with a stranger at the grocery store brought meaning to her life. Since those events were a daily fixture for her, she didn't realize the importance of even seemingly trivial interactions. When the anxiety finally became so great that it kept her isolated and immobilized, she didn't realize that those numerous interactions, no matter how trivial they may have seemed, were fuel for her soul.

All she could put into words was that she missed her old life and felt terribly ashamed for giving up on it. These days, she can barely bring herself to walk to the mailbox.

And so this once bold woman is isolated, depressed, and ashamed. She has lost the things that are most important to her. She often asks herself why a little bit of fear and a lot of depression has kept her from other people, but she just can't bring herself to leave the house while she feels so bad. She wishes she could go back to the day of the accident and erase that bit of history. She wishes she could make it all go away so that she could have her old life back.

The Past Is Not the Problem

Psychologists have a word for thoughts that seem to appear without cause or permission: *intrusions*. I would wager that most people, most of the time, don't mind intrusive thoughts because the thoughts are not offensive or unpleasant. *Don't forget the milk. That dress is ugly. I wish I had a giraffe.*

Some intrusions are less pleasant; some are downright disturbing, as were Penelope's recollections of the accident and the botched magic trick. She is like so many of us who wish that our thoughts would go away, or that we could simply erase pieces of our history from memory.

Consider the person who embarrasses himself by drinking too much in front of the family. That embarrassment is one more feeling from which he wants to escape, which only strengthens his desire to drink. He wishes he had never had the experience of drinking, or the feelings that led him to alcohol in the first place.

…Or consider the survivor of childhood abuse who has difficulty trusting others. The closer he gets to other people, the more uncomfortable and less trusting he feels. He curses his mind for holding on to history. Without it, he tells himself, he might be normal.

…Or the woman who lacked a dependable family and whose mind drew the conclusion that she wasn't good enough to deserve one. As she searches for a partner and a family of her own, her mind sabotages her with the thought that no one will want her. She resents her mind for being shaped by the past and wishes she had no desire for love.

Minds never forget the important lessons. Short of injury or illness to the brain, history cannot be erased. Worse still, history has a way of popping into memory at the worst possible times. It is while we prepare for a first date that we tend to recall our worst romantic experiences. We're most likely to recall our most traumatic public speaking gaffe just before giving a speech and our most shameful social blunder as we anticipate making new acquaintances at a cocktail party.

The Mind's Patterns of Avoidance

The mind is a "contextual machine"—that is, it's programmed to notice similarities from one environment in another, perhaps completely different, environment. It is all part of the ancient emotional circuitry designed to keep us out of harm's way. *If the small purple berries made you sick once, they'll make you sick again.* Armed with that knowledge, the mind defends us with a burst of disgust or revulsion designed to repel us from the berries. (Incidentally, that type of learned food aversion is universal among higher animals [Garcia, Hankins, and Rusniak 1976]. It's evidence that the brain is wired to acquire lessons directly related to survival more easily than other types of lessons.)

Unfortunately, our mind's use of history can drive us right over the cliff sometimes. When Penelope stays home to avoid another accident, she is responding as if the accident were about to recur. A good mind will try to control the environment whenever dangerous history seems to repeat itself. *Are those purple berries on that bush? Don't eat them!*

Even lab rats can recognize the context that has signaled danger in the past. It has long been known that a rat can be trained to press a lever after hearing a tone. All one needs to do to train the rat is to follow a tone with an electric shock. As soon as the rat stumbles onto the act of pressing a lever that prevents a shock, he will forever know to press the lever whenever he hears the tone. He has learned to control the environment when certain cues appear.

Interestingly, rats can even be trained to press the lever at regular intervals *without* a tone. If the shock comes at regular intervals, say every twenty seconds, but the shock can be prevented by pressing the lever shortly before the shock is due, rats will learn to press the lever with highly accurate timing (Sidman 1953). In this case, the rat is responding to a contextual cue from within—probably his sense that time has elapsed—rather than a warning from the environment. They're not so different from us.

Dear Penelope is doing precisely what the rat did when she chooses to stay home. She is avoiding the pain of another anxiety attack. Press the lever; avoid the shock. Just like the rat, we can be trained to avoid what we *think* is coming.

It makes sense to avoid a shock. Shocks are painful. Memories can also be painful, in their own way. When Penelope recalls the accident, she also recalls some of the panic she felt at the time, as well as the shame and embarrassment of botching her magic trick.

A good mind, being trained in the art of avoidance, will approach pain that comes from *inside* just as it manages pain that comes from *outside*: it will try to control and avoid it. *If purple berries make me sick, then I shall avoid them. If the memory of an accident makes me anxious, then I shall avoid the memory of the accident and anything that evokes that memory.*

When Penelope avoids the outside world, she's not avoiding an accident as much as she's avoiding the *thought* of the accident she already had.

This is perfectly logical from a certain point of view, but it does not work very well. Each time she avoids something in the outside world (her car, for instance) in order to prevent pain from within, she inexorably connects it to the memory of the accident.

Avoiding the car may insulate her from reexperiencing anxiety, but many things are associated with the car—like the garage, the street, and the grocery store. Those loose associations with the car (which is associated with the accident) can become directly associated with the accident as she avoids more and more things. They can all come to be perceived as part of the context that led to the accident in the first place. This is the ever-shrinking world that only our minds can create.

The obvious irony is that the garage, the street, and the grocery store pose no direct threat to Penelope. She's responding to painful thoughts and feelings or, stated more accurately, the fear that she might experience painful thoughts and feelings.

As we discussed earlier, there are other ways to avoid thoughts. Alcohol and drugs make them disappear for a little while. Sex and shopping distract us temporarily. Eating, gambling, and surfing the Internet can bring respite from the mind. These things may not be inherently destructive, but we can lose ourselves to them when we use them to avoid history, thoughts, and feelings.

Working that hard to avoid our own minds is dreary business. Waiting for thoughts to go away can take a lifetime.

The Mind's False Dilemmas

If only my thoughts and feelings would leave me alone, I could finally get on with my life.

I wager that any psychologist with more than a week's worth of experience has heard some variation of that statement. The assumption behind that sentiment is that the mind must be under control, with painful thoughts and feelings successfully locked away, before a person is able to live the life he or she desires. The sentiment comes in countless flavors:

* *I must get rid of these self-critical thoughts before I can find true love.*

* *I cannot do well on my exam unless I get rid of this self-doubt.*

* *I have to stop wanting food in order to lose weight.*

* *I could go to the gym if I only didn't feel so bad about myself.*

Truth is, these are all false dilemmas: *either* I can have the thoughts and feelings *or* I can live my life, but I cannot have both. Who can blame us humans for thinking that way? We are logical creatures. We're problem solvers who are used to putting our hands on problems. When we're talking about problems outside the skin, this approach works well:

* *I cannot drive to the store until I eliminate the problem with my car.*

* *I cannot wash the dishes until I fix the sink.*

* *I cannot build a house here until I clear away the trees.*

Humans are fabulous at knocking down obstacles. Because part of the function of thoughts and feelings is to create obstacles for us, it's natural to think that we must knock them down before moving on with our life. Penelope's anxiety, for example, has the perfectly legitimate function of preventing her from revisiting a location that was once dangerous. Her anxiety is a primitive and effective mental obstacle designed to further her survival.

Penelope's biggest problem is that her mind learned something new the day of the accident: traffic can be dangerous. She suffered to learn that lesson, and her mind isn't about to let her forget it. And thank goodness that forgetting isn't an option. What kind of survival-driven worry machine would disregard hard-won lessons?

Imagine an ancient hunter-gatherer tromping around the savanna when he has the painful experience of watching a companion die after eating poison berries. From that moment forward, he would have recalled the death of his friend at the mere sight of those berries—perhaps any type of berries. As painful as it may have been to watch the death of someone he depended on, and as painful as it surely was to recall that death, recalling the event is better than repeating it.

But no matter how painful they can be, thoughts and feelings are still just activities of the mind. They are not physical problems like broken-down cars, viruses, trees that must be cleared to make way for a house. They are not physical obstacles. They have only as much power as we give them.

Self-as-Content

Psychologist Steven Hayes has long been curious about the ways in which we respond to our thoughts. He has suggested one important factor that makes thoughts seem so powerful. It has to do with our view of history (Barnes-Holmes, Hayes, and Dymond 2001).

Penelope views herself and her thoughts in the typical fashion. She views herself, at least in part, as the sum of her history, thoughts, and feelings. She believes that as we go through life, we are like containers that get filled with a potluck of experiences—some good, some bad.

Like most of us, if you ask her to describe herself she'll tell you about things she's done: "I'm the daughter of a straight-laced accountant. I rebelled and became an entertainer." The structure of her answer has a certain temporal structure: *I* (here and now) *am a result of what happened when I was younger* (there and then).

Hayes calls this perspective *self-as-content*. I am the container for my experiences; my experiences fill me up and forever define me.

There are advantages to this perspective. For example, Hayes points out that this gives us a consistent frame of reference when we converse with each other. If you and I meet at a cocktail party, I can be confident that you will talk about yourself from the same perspective I will use: *I* (here and now) *did something* (there and then).

However, this perspective comes at a cost. It can lead us to label ourselves, either positively or negatively, in very limiting ways. For example, Penelope at one moment might believe the thought *I* (here and now) *am a good magician, because the audience applauded loudly* (there and then).

At a different moment, she might believe an entirely different thought: *I* (here and now) *am a terrible magician, because I had a traffic accident and became so upset that I botched a performance* (there and then).

Buying into either thought as if it were a factual, physical thing limits behavior. For example, if someone were to ask her out to lunch while she was having the "good magician" thought, Penelope might say yes because good magicians are allowed the confidence to go out in public. If she were in the midst of a "bad magician" thought, however, she might decline: *What business do I have being seen in public? I'm a failure.*

It is in these moments, when we are judging ourselves, that thoughts can feel absolutely factual. From a distance, we can see the arbitrary nature of Penelope's self-judgments. She's simply picking one piece of data and drawing a conclusion based on her current mood. She's losing the range of her experience and her own complexity. Worse, she's making decisions based on fleeting thoughts rather than doing what she really wants to do.

The long-term cost of self-as-content thinking is this: we're likely to believe that we are limited by our content, or that we cannot proceed until our content changes. Penelope believes that she cannot become a good magician until the memory of the traffic accident—and all that followed from it—disappears from memory. Only when it is no longer part of her content can she return to her old self. The obvious problem is that her history will never go away.

Self-as-Context: Another Option

We have an alternative to accepting the mind's false dilemmas and self-as-content. Rather than viewing ourselves as containers, holding too much of this history or not enough of that, we can begin to look at ourselves as the medium in which fleeting events take place. We are the environment for a thousand experiences, thoughts, and emotions. Hayes calls this perspective *self-as-context*. It doesn't work very well at cocktail parties, but it's great for mental health.

Self-as-context works like this: I am not merely the sum of my experiences. Rather, I am always in the present, here and now, going about my business. Sometimes I recall my history; sometimes I don't. I am always experiencing thoughts and emotions. But I am only the playground on which these things carouse for a short time. Soon enough, others will replace them. They do not define me any more than a heartbeat defines me. They are simply passing activities of the mind.

Hayes, Strosahl, and Wilson (1999) offer a useful metaphor to illustrate self-as-context. Imagine a chessboard that stretches out in all directions. There are black pieces and white pieces fighting against each other, working as teams. This is a game of war.

You can think of your thoughts and feelings as the chess pieces. Like the black team and the white team, we tend to imagine our thoughts and feelings as teammates. There are "good" feelings, like self-confidence and happiness, and "bad" feelings, like anxiety, fear, and sadness. Just as in chess, we pick the side that we want to win. We want the good feelings to defeat the bad ones, and so we mount our battle against the enemy. We try to eliminate it from the board.

There's a problem with this. Trying to eliminate something within us only makes it stronger. (Remember the monkeys?) The more we fight the enemy pieces, the bigger they become. It's a game that cannot be won.

Hayes asks, "What if you don't play one side or the other? What if you aren't the pieces or the player? What if, instead, you are the chessboard itself?"

When you choose a side, the game must be won, as if your life depends on it. But if you are the board, there is no reason to invest in the game. The board simply contains the pieces. It is the context in which the dynamics of the game exist. The game cannot exist without the board, but the board has no need to defeat one side or the other. From the board's point of view, there is no good team or bad team.

Self-as-context means viewing our internal experiences from the vantage point of the board. Rather than viewing myself (here and now) as good or bad because of some past experience (there and then), there is only this: me (here and now) experiencing a thought, a feeling, a memory.

Here's an exercise to help you develop your self-as-context skills. It will help you notice your judgments about your own thoughts.

Exercise: Noticing Judgments

Judgments about our thoughts are just like any other thoughts. They parade through our mind as if they were factual. **This thought is good. It can stay. That thought is bad. It must go**. When we choose sides on this chessboard of thoughts, we are only battling ourselves.

This exercise will help you notice judgments and emotional reactions to your own thoughts. It will help you notice when you choose sides: **this is a good thought; this is a bad thought.**

For this exercise, you will write down two thoughts—one on each side of a small piece of paper. On one side, write a thought that you have come to believe is good, such as a self-confident thought, or the memory of an achievement. It might be something like **I did a good job with a difficult customer at work** or **My clothes look nice today.**

On the other side, write a thought that you believe is bad. No need to make it **too** bad. Choose something mild like **I wish I had done more homework in high school** or **I am not a very good dancer**, but make sure the thought has a small amount of negative emotion attached to it. For the purposes of the exercise, it should be a thought that you don't enjoy.

Carry the piece of paper for a day or two in your wallet or purse, or some other place where you will stumble across it periodically. Whenever you happen across the paper, read one of the thoughts—whichever one presents itself at that moment—and notice your reaction to it. Does it make you smile a little bit? Do you want to stuff it back into your pocket so that you need not think about it?

Notice the judgment, and notice what you want to do about it. You might even notice yourself trying to place the paper back in your pocket so that you stumble onto the "good" thought next time.

Finally, accept the judgment as just one more thought in the parade, and move on. Just like any other thought, judgments are mere thoughts, and nothing more. These just happen to be thoughts to which we have attached evaluations. It is possible to carry them without being controlled by them.

For Penelope, being able to view her internal experiences without evaluation or judgment—that is, from the vantage point of the chessboard or self-as-context—might be the beginning of freedom. But there is more to be done. In the next chapter, we'll look at how and why her mind reacted as it did. If she is going to observe the chess game, it helps to understand how the game works.

Chapter 5

The Mind's Skewed View and Biased Memories

Fear is one of the most important things the mind does. It's a lifesaver when the mind correctly executes the act of fear. When the mind misapplies it, fear comes at a high cost.

Sometimes the mind learns a little too well, as in the case of panic attacks, an experience that someone in Penelope's position could easily begin to suffer.

Panics attacks are periods of intense fear lasting anywhere from fifteen seconds to several minutes. People often report feeling as if they're having a heart attack, they're going to die, or they're going crazy. Panic attacks usually include physical symptoms like heart palpitations and hyperventilation that intensify the fear. To make matters worse, sufferers of panic attacks frequently worry that they will look foolish or incompetent in front of others. A panic attack is one of the most painful experiences that the mind can offer.

The prevalence of panic attacks is difficult to calculate because many episodes go unreported, but we do know that more than one out of every fifty people has panic attacks frequent and severe enough to be diagnosed as panic disorder (Kessler et al. 2005). Though it's called different things in different places, symptoms similar to what we call panic occur across cultures (Hinton and Hinton 2002). Panic is an equal-opportunity, uniquely human experience.

It is also a grand illusion. During an attack, the mind and body react as if death is imminent when there is nothing in the immediate environment that poses a threat. Many people who experience panic attacks wonder if they're losing their sanity. After all, why on earth would an evolved mind do something so painful without a good reason?

The answer may lie in the fact that the systems within our modular brain sometimes find themselves at odds with one another. Panic occurs when structures deep within the brain—structures that don't have a window to the outside world—activate self-protective measures.

Take the *amygdala*. In fact, take two—they're small. The amygdalae are a pair of almond-shaped structures that lie deep within our brains as part of the limbic system, which is concerned with emotion and motivation. They play an important role in panic. For example, they can initiate panic when they sense that the blood has become too acidic, which usually indicates surplus carbon dioxide (Esquivel et al. 2010). That can happen, for example, when we become tense and hold our breath. Ideally, this acid-sensing system merely prompts us to take a breath, but the amygdalae are not known for nuanced responses when danger lurks. (Incidentally, some people are more prone than others to panic resulting from increased carbon dioxide in the blood.)

This part of the brain is also involved in a special kind of knowledge acquisition called *one-trial learning*, which are emotion-laden lessons learned from a single event: burn your hand once, and you will forever remember that stoves get hot.

Wouldn't it be wonderful to study a subject only once and enjoy instant recall for the rest of your life? Medical school, computer programming, and tax forms would be a breeze. Unfortunately, one-trial learning is reserved for lessons that are colored by powerful emotions like fear. The amygdalae can help us memorize dangers in a single lesson, as Penelope learned after one accident. After that accident, she knew that a certain intersection was unsafe. The *synaptic connections* (the junctions through which neurons communicate) that make up these new memories are actually stronger and more immediate than those of memories unrelated to fear (Ostroff et al. 2010).

What the Mind Fears and How It Responds

So why does any of this physiology matter? It illustrates the ways in which our primitive minds can be pitted against our higher, rational minds. Logically, Penelope is well aware that the intersection in which she had her accident poses no inherent danger, but through the magic of survival mechanisms like one-trial learning, her primitive mind works from a different base of knowledge. Her primitive mind "knows" that the intersection is life threatening.

Aside from direct threats to our physical safety, the mind speaks most strongly to us about dangers that historically have threatened our species. For example, children's minds are primed to make difficult visual distinctions between spiders and other bugs, including similar-looking ones like cockroaches (LoBue 2010).

In a similar way, the mind appears to have a natural aversion to isolation and social pain. Abandonment is one of the worst things that can happen to a person, and for a young person in earlier times it meant almost certain death. As you might expect, the mind seems to have adapted some specialized mechanisms to prevent isolation. When social relationships are threatened, damaged, or lost, some of the same brain systems involved in physical pain are activated.

This appears to be the mechanism behind the emotional pain we feel when we experience strained relationships (Eisenberger and Lieberman 2004). It's one of the many areas where the line between anxiety and depression is blurry. The activation of certain physical pain systems may be why the dog that's left alone howls so plaintively. It's the sound of a mind experiencing the miserable angst of social separation.

Humans also have a special form of suffering that other animals cannot experience. We can attach emotional content to thoughts, symbols, and memories in a unique way.

Say, for example, that I take my cat to the veterinarian, who gives her a shot of medicine. Cats hate shots, and so the next time I show her a hypodermic needle, she will resist and show signs of distress. She might shiver and howl, and her little heart will pound in her chest. Because she remembers the pain it caused, she will do whatever she can to get away from that needle before it strikes again.

When she responds that way, we can be certain that the cat has associated the needle with painful shots in the tushie. Humans operate the same way in the presence of a thing that has caused pain before. Nothing extraordinary there.

Here's the interesting part. Animals can be trained to report that they have experienced a painful event (by pushing a lever, for example). When they do so, there are no signs of distress. They don't howl and their hearts don't pound. Even though they are remembering pain, they seem as calm as if they were contemplating a sunny day.

A human, on the other hand, will show signs of distress when describing a past, painful experience, almost as if the thing itself is present, rather than the memory of it (Wilson et al. 2001).

Sometimes the memory of a painful event can evoke more distress than the actual event did. Just ask Penelope. Sometimes an imagined event can cause distress even though the person has never experienced it. If you've ever worried about your own death, you know what I mean.

These are some of the things the primitive mind fears. The mind has a simple response to pain and fear: avoid, avoid, avoid. And how does it persuade us to avoid things? By giving us the pain of anxiety and sadness. When we approach something dangerous—whether it's a particular intersection, social isolation, or even our own painful thoughts—the mind tries to smack us with one form of pain or another. When it comes to safety, the mind is all stick and no carrot. Systems like the amygdalae are regularly dishing out punishment in order to keep us safe.

As I'm sure you have noticed, the primitive mind does not have the most accurate view of the world, which means we're often getting smacked for dangers that aren't even present at the moment. There is a reason the mind has such a skewed view of things.

The Survival Value of Biased Recall

I try not to argue with other people's minds. I rarely argue with my own. The reason is that I can't compete. Minds are expert at remembering bad experiences, and they can always come up with one more example of why they are right. This may be no more evident than when we are trying to cheer someone up using logic and good sense, and their minds are having none of it.

You: "Why so glum, chum?"

Your friend: "I've finally realized that I'm good for nothing."

You: "What? Don't be silly. You're one of the most impressive people I know. You went to Harvard. You have a great job, and I don't mind saying you're good looking."

Your friend: "Good looking? With this nose? I don't think so. I barely scraped by at Harvard, and my job is basically meaningless. What kind of accomplishment is that? That proves how incompetent I am. Everyone else I graduated with is doing great things."

You: "What about that project you did in New York? That was a big deal."

Your friend: "Please. I was barely in the background. Everyone else did the work. I'm a fraud."

...and so the conversation will continue when we get drawn into arguing with a mind.

When the mind is in this mode, it doesn't matter how hard we try to prove it wrong. It can always find one more piece of evidence in its favor, no matter how irrational the conclusion. A mind in this mode can turn a Harvard education into evidence of failure. When a mind puts on the donkey brakes, there is no budging it. This is why I don't argue with minds.

As frustrating as it can be to encounter this type of thinking in someone else's mind or in our own, there is usually a reason for it. The mind does not invoke the donkey brakes simply out of belligerence. There is usually a reason having something to do with control.

It is not uncommon, for example, for a child who suffers abuse at the hands of their family to grow into someone who believes that their relationships—particularly intimate ones—are jinxed. Having suffered physical and emotional pain at the hands of people who should be trustworthy, a normal, healthy mind will go to work on this problem: What do I need to do in order to prevent this from happening again?

Minds like to control the outcomes of things, and they like to solve problems so those problems don't repeat. That's why our minds employ strategies such as rumination, their way of focusing our attention on complex problems. Some problems, like being abused at the hands of family members, have no easy explanations. It simply doesn't make sense to abuse family members.

This presents the mind with a terrible quandary. When there is no clear explanation for a problem, and therefore no reliable way to prevent it in the future, what's a mind to do?

Most sane and sensible minds will focus attention inward when no other answers are apparent. If there is no explanation in the world outside the skin, then the problem must exist inside the skin, our minds seem to think. The question *How can I prevent this in the future?* becomes *How did I cause this, and how can I change in order to prevent it from happening again?* If the problem is within us, then it can be identified and fixed—or so our control-starved minds seem to think.

Which brings us back to the mind's innate ability to find never-ending pieces of evidence against the self. The possibility that we might discover an answer within ourselves offers hope and a sense of control. The survivor of abuse may spend a lifetime marinating in self-observation and self-criticism, hoping to discover and repair whatever problem has so far prevented peaceful, safe relationships.

For most people, self-criticism is not a constant behavior. It comes and goes. But when it is present—when the mind is cherry-picking derogatory data—then arguing is as pointless as saying "calm down" to someone in the midst of a panic attack. It might even make things worse.

If you have noticed this tendency in yourself, don't feel bad. Humans in general seem prone to cherry-picking our data. It even happens in carefully designed research, when you'd least expect it. The body of knowledge that forms the social sciences is replete with a built-in flaw known as the *file drawer problem*. The result of this problem is that data are unintentionally filtered to support a specific outcome (Howard et al. 2009).

The file drawer problem works like this. Researcher A designs a study to determine whether people can read minds. His results suggest that people can read minds, and so he publishes his study and gains much attention. Meanwhile, researchers B, C, D, E, and F design similar studies and find no evidence of mind reading. Their studies go unpublished because, frankly, they're boring. Boring studies don't further the survival of a research department, and so they are placed in a file drawer, never to see the light of day.

The point is this: humans have a tendency to see information that furthers our survival and to disregard information with less survival value. In the academic world, that means publishing exciting studies that draw attention and money. With individuals, it means focusing on unpleasant lessons from the school of hard knocks.

Researchers have difficulty recognizing the file drawer problem (Rysen 2006), and so do we as individuals. That's why arguing with your friend in the interest of cheering him up can be so ineffectual. It's a battle against human nature; it's a battle against the design and function of the mind.

Even Penelope's mind fell prey to the file drawer problem. It focused on a single fender bender, ignoring the thousands of times she has driven through intersections without incident. She can thank her limbic system for that one-trial learning and flawless recall, and she can thank her mind for focusing on the information that had the greatest survival value. It was only doing its job.

How the Mind Makes Rules to Keep Us Safe

One-trial learning is a brilliant survival mechanism. Better our ancestors should have remembered the single time they barely escaped with their lives than the countless times they were perfectly safe. There is more survival value in remembering the single incident.

The same is true for the file drawer problem, which really isn't a problem where survival is concerned. Our ancestor who was on thin social ice would have been well served by recalling the times he made mistakes, so that he could avoid repeating them and being ostracized.

Fear and avoidance are just two of the things the mind uses to do what it does best: protect us. What could be simpler than fearing and avoiding dangerous things?

There are no free lunches in life. We pay a price for the privilege of carrying these mechanisms that our ancestors worked so hard to develop for us. Fear and avoidance can take on a life of their own, as they did with Penelope. The mind sometimes seems to believe that the more things we fear and avoid, the greater our chances of survival.

That logic was probably functional at one time, but the world isn't as dangerous as it once was. If I could get my mind to understand one thing, it would be this: most things are not a matter of life and death. Lighten up already, mind! For better or worse, that is not a message that my mind is willing or able to receive. Biology has its limits. That means that the mind is going to go about its business of protecting us, and if we're not careful, we can start to believe what it says. The more we allow the mind to control our behavior, the more entrenched we become in the kind of thoughts that are dominated by fear, anxiety, and depression.

A mind can be like a nervous dog in the backyard, barking frantically at every passing squirrel, and wearing a path at the back fence. Over time, dogs that are allowed to continue with that behavior become louder, more frantic, and more aggressive. As annoying and irrational as it may seem to others, their behavior makes sense from a dog's perspective.

That frantic, menacing behavior is the dog's response to its perception of a threat—with "perception" being the key word. Most of the things this dog barks at—squirrels, birds, and pedestrians—don't really pose a threat. Regardless, the frantic barking is self-reinforcing.

Each time the dog engages in a hysterical response, it notices a correlation between barking and the departure of the perceived threat. Any reasonable dog would conclude that his barking caused the intruder to leave, when in fact there was probably no relationship between the two events.

Minds behave in a similar way. Each time Penelope avoids leaving the house because she is afraid to do so, there is an unavoidable correlation between avoidance and the rewards that follow—she doesn't have an accident. Avoidance reinforces itself in two ways: escaping unpleasant experiences and gaining the comfort of safety.

This plays out in more subtle ways, too. Let's think back on our example of the person who was abused by her family and now struggles with thoughts such as *What did I do to cause this?* Treating that thought as if it had a factual basis—*I caused this*—turns the thought into the metaphorical dog barking at the back fence. It wears a path, and the behavior grows in strength over time.

Thoughts like *What did I do to cause this?* usually result in self-imposed rules that limit exposure to danger: *Don't let anyone get too close. Don't let them know too much or see the real you. Everyone is abusive until proven otherwise—and there's no real way to prove otherwise.*

Penelope's mind came up with rules, too: *Stay away from the intersection. Stay away from the street. Stay away from the car. Stay indoors.*

These two examples—Penelope, with her growing anxiety, and the woman who wonders how she caused others to abuse her—look different on the surface. But something very similar is happening within each person: the mind perceives danger, constructs rules to control exposure, and uses feelings like anxiety and depression as a punishment for breaking those rules.

Fear—combined with repetitive, self-negating thoughts—leads to an ever-shrinking world governed by ever-increasing rules. Rules can take over a mind like weeds invading an open field. Eventually, they can break our spirit.

Luckily, the dog that wears a path in the backyard can be trained, and so can we. That is not to say that the nature of the dog can be changed. Its urge to protect its territory cannot be eliminated, nor should it be. We need not defeat the dog in order to change its behavior in a way that makes everyone more comfortable, the dog included.

So how to proceed? How do we get our old behaviors back? How does Penelope get her life back? How does the survivor of abuse begin to create healthy relationships?

Well, we already know that trying to defeat the mind can create more fear, more avoidance, more anxiety and depression. And if we sit around waiting for the rules to change, we will be waiting for a very long time.

There is another option: break the rules.

Breaking the mind's rules can be difficult and uncomfortable. It helps to know why we're doing it, and that's where personal values come in. In the next chapter, we'll look at how clearly defined values can help free us from our own minds.

Chapter 6

Values and Action

Our minds devise rules to keep us safe. For the most part, this arrangement works fairly well. The first time we touch a hot stove, our minds create a useful rule for us to follow: don't touch hot stoves.

Clearly, however, there are times when the mind gets carried away. We see this in Penelope, whose mind is beginning to tell her that the world is so dangerous that she should remain in the safety of her home. Her mind is correct that the world is a dangerous place, but it's not too dangerous to enter. Furthermore, avoiding everything is not practical—at least not for her. She would rather go outside and bring joy to others than to waste away in the safety of her living room.

It's an odd and uniquely painful experience for Penelope. *She* wants to live her life; her *mind* wants her to hide. It's as if there is another entity inside her that has set up walls she never wanted. No wonder people in her position so often tell me that they feel like they're constantly fighting their minds.

In a way, that's not far from the truth. Being the modular organ that it is, the brain often has competing urges. The different systems of the brain quite literally compete with each other sometimes. Panic disorder is one example: the primitive mind is in a serious tizzy, sounding the alarm bells, while we in our higher minds recognize that there is nothing to panic about.

Rumination is another example of the mind competing with itself, as the brain shunts our mental resources toward whatever complex problem demands our attention. Even addictions can be seen as a mind competing with itself. We get caught in a powerful drive for short-term relief, even when we recognize the long-term costs. (We'll discuss this more in chapter 10.)

It is difficult to win an argument with the primitive mind because doing so often involves arguing with powerful emotional experiences. There is hope, though. We are also wired to see beyond those experiences, to find a way out, and to live our lives in spite of them. If that were not the case, you would not be reading this book.

Training the Mind to Tolerate the Pursuit of Values

Here's another reason to disengage from a battle with the mind: it's already battling itself. I'm not speaking metaphorically. Our brains have physical structures that appear to help us ignore messages from the primitive mind. For example, there is an area of our brains called the *anterior cingulate cortex* (ACC). One of its jobs is to act as intermediary between the panic-inducing limbic system and our cortex, the seat of our higher, rational minds.

Think of a courtroom battle, with our emotional, hyperreactive limbic system on one side and our calm, cool, logical cortex on the other. The ACC sits between them, acting as judge, deciding whether or not the panic systems rule the day (Frankland et al. 2004). Like a courtroom, precedent matters to the ACC. The more often the primitive mind has prevailed in the past, the more likely it is to have its way once again.

Here's the good news: the ACC can be strengthened to more often rule in the direction of our *values*—the principles and standards that drive us toward meaningful action—as determined by our higher, rational minds. This is one of the things that happens when we learn to manage anxiety disorders.

Strengthening the ACC doesn't involve stopping the primitive mind from giving us anxiety. We don't need to stop it. Instead, we can simply practice responding differently when the primitive mind speaks. With practice, we can learn to choose to respond from our higher mind rather than being bossed around by the primitive mind.

The fact that our primitive minds exist and speak to us is not necessarily a problem. The problem is overrehearsal in the wrong direction. Each time we buy into experiences like rumination, anxiety, or procrastination, we strengthen those behaviors in the primitive mind. Buying into our thoughts also weakens our ability to see past them.

Remember the dog at the back fence? He was wearing a path in the yard, and making himself and everyone else miserable with his hysterical reactions to perceived threats. The problem feeds itself. Over time, the dog will become increasingly anxious and aggressive.

Well-trained dogs aren't allowed to let their hysteria rule the day. A dog can be trained to act calm and cool even when doing so is in violation of its impulses. In dogs, as in people, impulses and emotions are not rules to be followed.

At our house, when the dog becomes frantic at the sound of the doorbell, we don't give in to the hysteria. Nor do we try to eliminate her protective instinct—why would we? Instead, we thank her for being a good watchdog and assure her that we have the situation under control. She still gets excited and even frightened sometimes, but she has learned to stand back and let the humans handle the situation.

You can think of this as top-down management. Biology compels her to guard the perimeter, and we are thankful for that, but we do not allow her to work herself into a hysterical frenzy at every harmless event.

If you'll pardon the comparison, we can deal with our primitive minds in a similar way. The more we allow our minds to control our behavior (for example, by avoiding a situation that poses no real threat, as Penelope did), the stronger our minds become and the more influence they have over us (Schlund et al. 2010).

The reverse is also true. We can take our minds by the proverbial hands, move forward in the service of our values, and train ourselves not to give in to the mind's every demand. Police, soldiers, and firefighters do precisely that. They practice not reacting on impulse, but instead responding in the most useful way.

The brain can physically change to reflect that type of training. For example, fear-laden memories can last a lifetime thanks to structures like the amygdalae. But the impact of those memories can decrease as we strengthen systems like the ACC that act as a buffer between us and the impulses of our primitive minds (Poulos et al. 2009). In other words, we can train ourselves to override the impulses that get us into trouble, just as a dog can be trained to override its impulses.

With practice, it gets easier, but it does take work. We begin by developing values as our guide. After all, if we are going to disobey the mind, it helps to understand why we're doing it, and to have an alternative in place so that we know what to do instead. Values can provide both the reason for disobeying the mind and the guideposts to our decision-making.

The Higher Mind

Until now, we've been talking about the mandates of the primitive mind. Let's focus for a moment on the other side of things—our higher, rational minds, where values come from. While our minds are acting *as if* there is something about which to be panicked, depressed, ruminative, or angry, we can cause our higher minds to act *as if* those thoughts and emotions don't matter any more than a fenced barking dog matters to a squirrel sitting safely in a tree. Let's call that *psychological flexibility*.

Behavioral psychologists use the term psychological flexibility to describe the willingness to respond to what's happening in the environment rather than what's happening in the mind. The mind inherently wants to adhere to rigid rules based on actions that have reduced pain in the past. A psychologically flexible response is grounded in the present moment, and it sometimes requires the willingness to endure discomfort in the pursuit of higher values. It is guided by values and wisdom rather than insistent thoughts and feelings (adapted from Baer 2010).

Rather than trying to suppress the mind, we can fight a different battle. We can fight for the flexibility to live our lives as we wish, recognizing that the mind hopes to constrain us but knowing that we need not be constrained.

The pursuit of flexibility takes place in countless small ways. Perhaps you are at a cocktail party, where your mind wants to insulate you from social rejection. It compels you, by punishing you with anxiety, to keep a low profile. It wants to impose rules to keep you safe: *Don't talk to strangers. Don't make eye contact. Spend time hiding in the bathroom.* However, it is possible to act *as if* you are an outgoing, gregarious person despite your primitive mind acting *as if* you face great danger by doing so.

The rub is that the mind imposes rules by punishing us. We quite literally feel bad or uncomfortable when we break the mind's rules. It stands to reason, then, that we had better have something pretty powerful in our arsenal to help us overcome that discomfort.

That secret weapon is our values. When we have a clear understanding of the ideals that we hold to be important, we then have a sound and compelling reason to go against the mind—to act *as if.* A clear understanding of our values can give us the strength to be flexible when the mind is demanding unreasonable and costly constraint.

Pursuing values will always, eventually, evoke some discomfort. If you struggle with anxiety, then moving toward freedom will increase your anxiety—for a little while. If depression has made your world smaller, then expanding your world may remind you of the reasons for your depression and make you sadder—for a little while.

Freedom has that effect. This is one of the most basic and frequently recurring questions in life: do I pursue freedom, or do I play it safe? Pursuing freedom and playing it safe both have costs, and both bring their own form of discomfort. But I believe it is a basic human yearning to be free, to have choices, and to embrace life with flexibility rather than to hide safely in the shadows. Flexibility doesn't mean freedom from pain; it means having the freedom to choose your destiny.

When fighting for our freedom, it helps to understand what, exactly, we are fighting for.

Finding Your Values

How would you prefer to spend your limited time on this planet? Ideally, would you spend it in the service of your family? Your job? Your religion or political cause? If you had only one year to live, what parts of your life would become most important to you? How would you want people to speak about you in your absence?

If you struggle to answer those questions, you're not alone. Many people have difficulty with them.

In theory, defining one's own values should be simple. Just name what's important to you—problem solved! But in practice, it can be more difficult than that. In my clinical experience, some people struggle with narrowing down what's most important. It *all* seems important, they say. Others have difficulty identifying anything that really matters to them.

Even when values are clear, the demands of life pull us in other directions, as do our own minds. The primitive mind doesn't give a whit about our lofty values. Often the mind seems flatly opposed to them. A person may want to become a brilliant actress, while her mind tells her to stay off that damned scary stage. A values-driven existence often involves direct contact with that kind of distress. Each of us must eventually choose between values and comfort.

Hayes, Strosahl, and Wilson (1999) liken values to directions on a map. A person can travel west but can never arrive at "west." There is no endpoint. Where values are concerned, we can always take one more step in the right direction no matter how well or how poorly we're performing at the moment. Values help direct our behavior in the present moment; *goals*, by contrast, are future-oriented intentions. We can meet our goals along the way, but we will never finish living in the service of our values.

Clearly defined values are part of the antidote to an overbearing mind. In order to function in our favor, values are best stated in terms of how we would like to *behave* rather than what we would like to *have*. For example:

"I want to be an excellent mother," rather than "I want my kids to love me."

"I value being an effective advocate for my political cause," rather than "I want my cause to win."

Having a clear sense of the person we want to be guides us in the moment-to-moment struggle to coexist with our own minds. Clearly stated values can guide us when we don't know how to respond to an overbearing mind. The key is to start with small behaviors. The following exercise will help you "think small" in big ways!

Exercise: Life Is in the Details

In order to help identify values, psychologist Kelly Wilson and his colleagues (2010) have identified ten domains that are important to many people:

_____ Family relations (other than marriage or parenting)

_____ Marriage/couple/intimate relationships

_____ Parenting

_____ Friendships / social relations

_____ Employment

_____ Education/training

_____ Recreation

_____ Spirituality

_____ Citizenship / community life

_____ Physical well-being

_____ Other _____

Which of these matter the most to you? Are there areas of your life that are not listed here, but are important to you? Dr. Wilson suggests assigning a numerical value of importance to these domains, with 1 being "not important" and 10 being "extremely important." Before you go on to the next exercise, take some time—as much as you need—to consider which areas are most important to you in life.

Record the numerical value in the space before each category. If all or several of the categories have high numbers, see if you can cut the list in half, and then in half again until you are left with the domains that are most important to you.

As you assign values to the domains in Dr. Wilson's list, try to define their importance in terms of your own behavior. For example, if intimate relationships are most important, describe **how you would like to behave** in an intimate relationship, rather than how you would like to benefit, how you would like to feel, or how you would like the other person to act.

Once you have narrowed down your list to the most important domains, the next question is this: are you living in the service of your values? If your answer is no, have the demands of life, or the demands of your own mind, taken you off course? If so, how do you get back on track?

Living in the service of values need not be a major production. Suppose you value being an outstanding parent. It may not require grand gestures such as daily trips to the zoo or the most expensive toys and clothes. Instead, it may be much more meaningful to think about simple, meaningful behaviors. Make it a point each day, for example, to call your child from work, to read a story, or to make her laugh. Life is in the details, and values-driven parenting may be simply a question of simple, thoughtful connection with the kiddo in many small ways. Values-driven behavior can be defined by answering this question: am I being the person I want to be at this moment?

Losing Track of Values

It's common to notice ourselves acting inconsistently with our own values, and that is quite normal. Joanne Dahl and her colleagues (2009) outlined three of the most common traps that interfere with values-based action.

1. **Avoiding aversive thoughts and feelings.** The more meaningful a thing is to us, the more risk it holds. The person who wants to become an outstanding actress can't pursue that value without risking embarrassment and the sense of failure—after all, if she didn't care about acting, it wouldn't matter to her if she chewed the scenery. A good mind will try to protect her from the sense of failure by compelling her to avoid the stage with thoughts like *You'll be ready to act as soon as you get rid of this anxiety.* And so she can get lost in an endless attempt to master her anxiety while her acting skills languish. It's one of life's dirty tricks that avoiding discomfort often means forgoing our values. This budding actress may need to embrace her anxiety in order to seek what matters most. No one said pursuing values was easy.

2. **Pursuing secondary rewards such as admiration or rank.** Rewards like money, position, or admiration are wonderful and can make life exciting, but these things are not the same as values. For example, someone who values education can strive for high grades, but doing so may not make him the best student he can be. The danger in confusing the two is that secondary rewards (such as grades) are transient. We can be left feeling empty and dissatisfied during the dry spells, and ultimately we can veer off course from our values in the raw pursuit of secondary reinforcement. Someone who values education might very well find that being the best student possible does not always correspond with high marks. It may actually involve sacrifices along the way. But in the end, the pursuit of values will be more meaningful than a report card, which will soon enough be forgotten. Dr. Dahl and her colleagues offer a few guiding questions to distinguish between the pursuit of values and the pursuit of secondary goals:

If you had all the success you wanted, what would you do with your life then?

If you had an influential position right now, what would you use it for?

What would you do if you were suddenly happy and secure?

3. **Keeping up appearances.** Sometimes we lose sight of our values because we are simply caught up in doing what others expect of us. This is a particularly alluring trap when pleasing others feels good. Acting to please others can appear to be consistent with our values, but the function is quite different. It places our behavior under the influence of others. When that happens, we are no longer pursuing our own values, but living in the service of another master.

Acting inconsistently with our values is not the end of the world. It is probably more normal than not. If acting in the service of our values were easy, if it were pain-free, then everyone would do it almost all of the time.

Living up to our values to the best of our ability requires a good bit of self-monitoring.

I hope you'll spend some time on this topic before moving on. Defining values is no academic exercise. In later chapters, we'll be discussing some specific ways in which the mind works against us. Pursuit of values will be one of our most important antidotes to the mind's insistent and sometimes painfully protective nature.

Control Your Life, Not Your Mind

Many things in daily life can interfere with the pursuit of our values. But more often than not, in my experience, it is our own minds that keep us from pursuing what's most important to us. Why? Because doing so involves great risk. If we seek to be an ideal parent, we risk that our children may turn out poorly. If we seek to create an ideal marriage, we risk that it may one day end abruptly. If we seek physical fitness, we risk that our bodies will fail us. Pursuing our values usually puts us in contact with our greatest fears—at least for a little while, and usually when we're returning to our values after neglecting them.

The good news is, we don't stay afraid of things forever. We get used to things. The more we move toward something that seems threatening, the less threatening it becomes (Van Bockstaele et al. 2010). The more we move in the direction of our values, the less threatening the risks become. You can be sure that when Penelope is in the midst of one of her artful performances, the risk of failure is small in her mind. She is connected to her audience, alive, and full of joy. She may experience the niggling fear of making a mistake, but it is only when she neglects her values and stays home instead of performing that she perceives herself a failure in a much larger sense.

Penelope would be wise to begin breaking the rules her mind has imposed on her. If she wants freedom, she must be willing to fight for her values rather than fighting against her mind. She must be willing to drag her mind, kicking and screaming if necessary, back into the world. Once it's out in the world for a while, it will probably adjust. Even if it doesn't, she at least will have her life back, and she will become more skilled at ignoring her mind. Having a firm grasp of her values—understanding *why* she is violating her mind's rules—will make it much easier to withstand the protestations from her primitive mind.

Using the observational skills we built in earlier chapters (the racetrack metaphor, "I'm experiencing the thought," the chessboard metaphor, and the like), she can learn to watch her mind as if from a distance. She can reclaim her life in a way that may seem counterintuitive at first: change the behavior, and the mind may follow. For example, if she disobeys her mind's rule that says, *Don't drive!* she will probably experience an increase in anxiety. Eventually, however, that anxiety will begin to subside. In other words, her reluctant mind will begin to follow her lead. Living in the service of values often means acting in opposition to our own thoughts; it also means being uncomfortable sometimes.

In the Life Is in the Details exercise above, you identified your values and the ways in which you would like to behave in those valued domains. Now let me ask you a slightly more challenging question: are you acting in the service of your values? If you are, how consistently are you doing this?

What would you discover if you reflected on your activities for the last week? Would you notice yourself acting in accordance with your values, or would you see something else driving your behavior?

If you find that your behavior has not been consistent with your values, I'm willing to bet that you have simply fallen into other habits—habits based on rules written by a protective mind. That happens to all of us at one time or another. Yet, on some level, we continue yearning to live out our values and feel fully alive.

When Penelope's world became increasingly smaller after the accident, the number of rules increased and her habits changed. Her mind told her, *That place is unsafe,* and *This activity is off-limits.* She moved away from what she valued most. When she decides to take her life back, she will need to break the rules that have come to define her new reality. But don't worry; breaking our own rules is almost never as bad as we think it will be.

Consider the person who wants to lose weight and improve her health but is held in place by the thought *I'm not the kind of person who goes to the gym.* The easiest way to become the kind of person who goes to the gym is to simply go to the gym a few times. It may be awkward at first, it may feel fake— feelings like that are part of the richness of life—but soon enough she will make friends and find her way around. With a bit of consistent rule breaking, she will become the kind of person who goes to the gym.

Penelope presently doesn't regard herself as the kind of person who drives to the store. It's against the rules. But the more she breaks those rules, the easier it will become, especially if she breaks the rules in the service of bringing joy to others, which is one of her primary values.

Deciding to follow your values sometimes means dragging your mind against its will into new behaviors. It will fight back. It will give you anxiety, sadness, unpleasant thoughts, and maybe even physical discomfort. But it can only protest. It cannot hurt you, and soon enough your mind will adapt. Here are a few strategies for getting started on values-driven action:

* Stay in touch with your values. Write about them; talk about them. Simply writing about what's important to you is enough to help you get moving when your mind is gripped by inertia (Kanter, Busch, and Rusch 2009). The more you understand about your values, the more easily you can justify breaking your mind's rules.

* Start small. If you value becoming physically fit, you don't need to run a marathon. Setting the bar too high when you're unsure of your current capabilities may set you up for failure. Start with something nonthreatening like walking for ten minutes daily on a treadmill. You may find that your mind comes to expect it and even look forward to it.

* Take one step at a time when you're trying to get moving. Sometimes the thought of values-driven action can be overwhelming, so don't focus on the big picture. If you're trying to get to the gym, start out by simply putting your shoes on. Next, move your body out the front door of your house. And so on. Before you know it, you'll be at the gym and working up a sweat—and your mind won't even have seen it coming.

* Use prompts. Values-consistent action requires new habits. Use notes, alarms, and other reminders to keep you moving. Since the new behaviors may be a violation of the rules, your mind may conveniently forget.

* Follow your plan, not your mood. Your mind will not make it easy to follow your values, particularly when depression is present. Form a plan and follow it whether you feel like it or not. Don't wait until you feel like following it (Kanter, Busch, and Rusch 2009).

* Don't confuse thinking and preparation with action. Worrying about going to the gym or buying a nice outfit for the gym is not the same as *going* to the gym. Minds often confuse thinking with action.

* In pursuit of values, try to focus on how you want to be ("I want to live a healthy lifestyle") rather than what you do not want ("I don't want to be fat.")

* Know that the mind will try to resist change. You are leaving safety and embracing risk. You are calling into question your definition of self, breaking the rules your mind has come to associate with safety, stability, and sweet predictability. It will fight back—for a little while.

* Know that there are no failures in trying to establish new habits. Think of it as an experiment. If you don't get what you want, ask why and troubleshoot (Martell, Dimidjian, and Herman-Dunn 2010). If you didn't make it to the gym today, what got in the way? Name it so that it won't sneak up on you again.

* Keep in mind that following your values is no guarantee of happiness. It only guarantees a life with meaning.

* Remember that it's normal to lose track of your values.

* Finally, control what you can. You can't always control your mind, but you can manage your behavior in the world. If your mind won't allow happiness at the moment, you can at least move in the direction of your values. Your mind can tell you what to feel, where to go, or what to do, but you don't have to obey.

Breaking the mind's rules can come with a disorienting mix of emotions—pride, shame, exhilaration, or anxiety, to name a few. This next exercise will help you to see beyond the emotional reactions and stay focused on the pursuit of values.

Exercise: Breaking the Mind's Rules

Breaking the mind's rules can be disorienting. This exercise will help you stay on track by helping you to notice the consequences (both pleasant and unpleasant) of acting on your values. Often these consequences slip by unnoticed. Your task is to identify the consequences of the small acts that you do in pursuit of your values.

For example, suppose your mind insists on the safety of being a wallflower at the next party you attend, while your values urge you to seek more connection with people. See if you can identify the specific rules your mind has made for you being a wallflower. Does your mind urge you to look busy as you examine a magazine? Hide out in the bathroom? Converse only with people you already know?

Once you've identified the rules, break one of them. Start small. The size or importance of the rule doesn't really matter. The task is to notice what happens as you go against your mind.

Put words to the thoughts and feelings that build as you prepare to break the rule. Next, try to notice how you feel during the act of breaking the rule. Finally—and this is the most important part—notice how you feel after you break the rule.

Chances are, you will eventually feel pretty good after breaking one of your mind's rules in pursuit of your values, but that pleasure is sometimes overshadowed by the discomfort of the experience. It's normal to feel ambivalent, so let some time pass before you pass final judgment on the act. On balance, was it worth it? Would you do it again?

The Trap of Waiting for Thoughts and Feelings to Change

More than anything, Penelope wanted to escape her trap of anxiety. There are countless numbers of us in a similar position. We want freedom from whatever prison our minds have built. Many of us in that position labor under a common assumption: we will be unable to reclaim our lives until we have changed our moods, our thoughts, our anxiety, and so on. We may even believe that we *must* remain trapped until we feel better about ourselves, that only after our unwanted thoughts and feelings have been eradicated can we move forward.

In reality, waiting for thoughts and feelings to change only increases the intensity of the problem. Penelope, for example, will probably become more anxious about having anxiety, and more depressed and ashamed about failing to pursue her values.

It's an insidious trap. We can spend a lifetime waiting for thoughts and feelings to change. But the truth is, we need not wait for our mind's permission to move forward.

The bad news for Penelope is that there is no way out of her proverbial quicksand without experiencing pain. The good news is that the pain is something of an illusion. Nothing that her mind gives her in protest can actually hurt her. Let's take a closer look at some of the internal experiences—resistant thoughts and resistant feelings—she may encounter as she reclaims her life.

Resistant Thoughts

Along with her mind telling her she's no longer the kind of person who makes a splash in the world, Penelope will have to deal with the inertia that a mind develops during periods of neglected values.

We tend to believe what we hear ourselves saying and see ourselves doing. Over her period of inactivity, Penelope has rehearsed countless times her thoughts about the dangers of the world. As odd as it may sound, she may actually experience the vague thought that she would be doing something wrong by changing her behavior in the direction of her values.

The mind has a tendency to confuse our history with our values. It tends to believe that what we have been doing all these years is what matters most to us. It's comfortable, familiar, and predictable. Pursuing her values may require her to sit with the thought that her new behaviors are uncomfortable.

Her attempts at flexibility may also raise shameful thoughts that her recent behavior and the assumptions she has built about the world are wrong. The mind doesn't like to be wrong when it has invested heavily in a set of

91

behaviors. Penelope might do well to remember that sometimes it feels good to be wrong, especially when being wrong can get a person's life back on track.

Her well-functioning mind will also give her memories of the accident in the service of making her more vigilant and preventing a repeat. That, in turn, may lead to resistant feelings like anxiety.

Resistant Feelings

Exposing herself to the things she has been avoiding all this time will most certainly evoke anxiety for Penelope. Her mind will try desperately to warn her that she is putting her survival at stake, and her anxiety will probably spike. That spike in anxiety cannot hurt her, and it will not last.

Forcing our minds to face anxiety-provoking stimuli is a bit like breaking a toddler of the temper-tantrum habit. If a child becomes accustomed to getting his way by use of temper tantrums, he comes to expect that the next temper tantrum will be as effective as the previous one. If the temper tantrum does not work, he will try harder—maybe a lot harder, with a much bigger tantrum. But soon enough, with consistent training from the adults around him, he will learn that tantrums are no longer effective and drop the behavior. He may spontaneously try tantrums again on occasion, but as long as the response is consistently nonreinforcing, the tantrums will dissipate.

The danger with breaking the tantrum habit is in giving in during the tantrum spike. If the adults acquiesce when the child is increasing his tantrum intensity, then the child learns an important lesson: the small tantrums no longer work; getting my way now requires a *big* tantrum. The parents will now have to work that much harder to break the next tantrum.

Penelope will do well to remember this during the spikes in anxiety she is likely to encounter. She will be far better served by riding out the spikes before retreating. If she retreats during a spike in anxiety, she will have to work that much harder next time she makes the attempt.

Facing the world again may bring sadness by reminding her of all she has given up. She may face thoughts of relationships in decline, shows that she never performed, and how much she misses bringing joy to others. Thoughts like those may take her mind down the same old ruminative path that contributed to her immobility. Her mind will probably want to spend immense resources figuring out what went wrong.

Perhaps more thinking is the last thing Penelope needs. Perhaps it doesn't matter what went wrong as much as it matters that she simply get moving once again. The habit-changing techniques listed in the previous section may be far more useful. Action may be far more helpful than anything her mind has to offer at this point.

Penelope may experience a spike in sadness as she encounters the people and places she has missed out on. Each time she hears "Where have you been? We've missed you!" she may experience a little jab of shame. But as her life comes together again, all of those pleasant little interactions will begin to add up. The more she moves about in the world in pursuit of her values, the easier it will be for her to keep moving.

Take Your Mind with You on the Road to Valued Living

Why bother arguing with a mind? It can outgun us with emotion and it can always outmaneuver us with one more piece of evidence. Its job is survival, not happiness, and that isn't about to change.

Rather than battling our minds, we can strive for an existence that has meaning, taking our minds along for the ride with all of their anxiety, rumination, and worry. Clearly defined values can provide the motivation to drop the battle against the mind, the reason to disobey the mind, and the guidance to create a life of meaning.

In the next section, we'll look at some of the more sophisticated ways in which the mind tries to keep us out of harm's way, including ways in which the mind can win any argument—*if* we allow ourselves to be drawn into an argument against it. All those generations that have come and gone, evading dangers we no longer face, have left the mind with some nifty techniques for survival. Unfortunately, those same survival techniques can drag us away from our values and into the quicksand of battling our own thoughts and feelings.

These minds of ours need to be watched, but they do not need to be defeated. To the contrary, I believe we should be grateful for the protection they provide. *And* we should live our lives as we wish, in accordance with our values.

Of course, a good mind may not sit idly and tolerate our disobedience. A good mind will use all the tools at its disposal to force our compliance, and that's the topic of the next section. So gather up your mind—the parts you like, and the parts you don't—and bring it along as we expose some of the mind's more advanced techniques for keeping us safe.

Part 3

Four Ways Our Minds Coerce Us—and What We Can Do About Them

The swinging weight at the end of a pendulum is called a *bob*. In an ideal environment, the bob will swing as far in one direction as it swings in the other. Bobs can swing a little, or bobs can swing a lot.

Willingness to experience both the good and the bad in life is like the width of a pendulum's arc. If we want to experience great joy, then we must be willing to experience pain and loss at the other extreme. One doesn't come without the possibility of the other; the pendulum swings equally wide in both directions.

I believe that the human spirit craves freedom, a life of meaning, and richness of experience. At the core of our inquisitive and adventurous species is an innate willingness to gamble on happiness and let the pendulum swing wide in both directions.

The primitive mind, however, has other plans. It doesn't want a wide range of experience; it doesn't care about our values or our happiness. It wants the pendulum to swing in a small, safe arc. That way, we won't get hurt.

For the human spirit, that safe zone represents stagnation. It is where depression, rumination, avoidance, and anxiety live. If we're not paying attention, a good mind will use well-worn and effective techniques to still the pendulum and keep our range of experience within the safe zone. Those tricks of the mind, and what to do about them, are the topic of this section.

Chapter 7

That Was Then and This Is Then

No one ever said, "I forgot that stoves get hot. I knew it at one time, but it slipped my mind."

There was a time in each of our lives when stoves posed no threat, as far as we knew. They were big, harmless boxes that sat in the kitchen, ripe for climbing just like any other piece of furniture. Then, whether through direct or indirect experience, we learned of the dangers they pose. We once believed that they were safe, but things change—that was then and this is now. Minds are forever altered by painful experiences.

That was then and this is now doesn't work very well in reverse. Lessons about survival are not easily forgotten. If all the stoves in the world were suddenly rendered impotent, our minds would still bristle at the idea of slapping our hands down on a burner coil. We could try to convince our minds that stoves are no longer dangerous, but no healthy mind will take our word for it. It will tell us—again and again—*that was then and this is then*.

But it is a fact that some things in our lives are no longer dangerous. It is not true for stoves, or bears, or speeding cars, but it can be true in relationships. Things change, and what once threatened our survival might now be safe. The mind, designed to survive in a more primitive and physically dangerous environment, doesn't easily grasp *that was then and this is now* when it involves learning that a thing is no longer dangerous. Just ask Andy and Meg.

What Meg Doesn't Know About Andy

After five years of marriage to Andy, Meg is beginning to wonder if it is going to work. It is not that she doesn't love him—she does—she simply wonders if the two of them will ever break out of the pattern into which they've fallen. She is loath to imagine herself late in life, having the same old arguments that they repeat over and again. Meg would tell you that Andy is the sweetest guy in the world, until they get into an argument. That's when he seems to completely withdraw from her.

Their most recent argument concerned the dog. When no one was home, the clever mutt managed to steal a fresh loaf of banana bread that Andy had left sitting too close to the edge of the counter. Meg came home to discover a broken plate, a few crumbs on the floor, and a shame-faced dog hiding in the bedroom. Meg was angry, not so much at the loss of the bread as with Andy's absent-mindedness.

When Andy came home, he could sense Meg's anger before he saw her. Perhaps he noticed subtle cues about the situation—the missing bread, the sudden realization that the dog may have once again stolen food from the counter, or maybe the fact that Meg didn't greet him as she usually does. Whatever the cue, Andy had become skilled at recognizing the early warning signs of trouble, for reasons we will discuss shortly. He became immediately anxious about the impending argument, and more than a little resentful that his wife had become so difficult to live with.

This pattern had become familiar to Andy. It started as soon as Meg began bringing problems to Andy's attention. Whenever she did so, he seemed not to care. His attention would wander, he would give noncommittal answers, and he would generally act bored and annoyed at the conversation. That, in turn, left Meg feeling frustrated. The more he would disengage from the conversation, the more she would pursue and try to force him to participate.

As Meg heard Andy arrive that day, her minor frustration about the bread grew into anxiety about the looming argument (there was no denying that the bread was gone) as well as anger at the thought that she had been shortchanged in her marriage. Where had her kind and caring husband gone?

Though they each tried to skirt the argument, Meg found herself asking Andy why he had left the bread within the dog's reach. Andy, in turn, made a feeble attempt to defend himself, then became silent and sullen, acting as if he didn't care about her. Just as they had each feared, they lost themselves to the pattern that had become so ingrained.

Underlying this pattern was something that Meg didn't know about Andy. His seemingly sullen, uncaring behavior wasn't a chance development. It was not new, and it was not intended to evoke her frustration. Quite the contrary. It was old behavior that had served him well earlier in life, protecting him from people who were angry.

Andy grew up with a mother who drank heavily. She was never physically abusive, but alcohol made her moods and her words unpredictable. Andy never knew when she would fly into a rage. Sometimes she shouted at Andy's father; sometimes Andy was the target. When she imagined that Andy had done something unacceptable, she would berate him, and then send him to his room. Frequently, she called him stupid and careless.

Young Andy was never able to predict what would send her into a drunken rage. Things that would anger her on one day would earn praise the next, and vice versa. That's a recipe for an anxious kid. He tried to follow the rules, but they changed from day to day. His father was little help, retreating into his study whenever she became irate, leaving Andy to fend for himself.

Luckily, Andy's mind was there to protect him. It gave him two invaluable survival skills. First, he became adept at discerning the early warning signs—an empty wine glass on the counter, a subtle shift in his mother's mood, or the tense quietude that took place when she was pondering an imagined insult or injustice. Second, he learned to get out of the way.

Whenever he was able to predict her anger, he would hide in his room before it appeared.

But sometimes he missed the warning signs, and this is where Andy's history intersects with Meg.

Whenever young Andy found himself on the receiving end of an angry, incoherent lecture, he would practice perfect deference: he would become silent and avert his gaze, not daring to speak for fear that any response might evoke even more anger and insults. He hated being called stupid by his own mother, and he came to believe that it was true. He learned that submissive deference was the shortest route to the safety of his bedroom.

Andy's young mind did precisely what it was meant to do. It increased his odds of survival by placating an angry loved one. Now, all these years later, his mind is still using the same old strategy in response to Meg's frustration, even though the submissive deference that was once effective is now counterproductive. He wants to speak, but it feels as if his mind has shut down his ability to form words.

Meg perceives his deference as callousness, and so she becomes even more frustrated, which evokes more deference from Andy, which in turn increases Meg's frustration, and so on. Andy's mind is digging quite a hole, with all the best intentions.

History Fades, but It Never Vanishes

Andy's mind seems to be doing what most minds will do when a survival strategy is failing. *Try more! Do it harder!* Even though the old strategy is clearly failing him, minds turn to history in times of stress. *If it worked before, do it again.*

Numerous people have told me they wish their histories would simply go away. More specifically, they want *some* of their history to go away. They want to keep the good memories and lose the painful ones.

Our minds gather history whether we like it or not. Even if we don't recall specific events, experience shapes our minds. In chapter 2, we looked at implicit learning, which is the mind's process of gathering information and guiding our decisions without our awareness. Part of the mind's job is to compel us toward experiences that have worked well in the past, and away from experiences that have historically caused pain. History—especially the painful variety—never goes away.

The way our minds use history and memory fuel a couple of specific problems. First and foremost, memory is fallible. Where history is concerned, the mind simply can't always be trusted. Perhaps that's due to the fact that the mind does not record events like a tape recorder, but instead selectively reconstructs them based on what it believes to be the most important features of events (Lin, Osan, and Tsien 2006). Sometimes it insists that we act (against our own best interests) on the history that has the strongest emotion attached to it, and sometimes the mind flat out misleads us about what we have experienced.

Memory is also affected by mood. For example, a depressed mind tends to overgeneralize and misremember autobiographical events (Liu et al. 2010). It might judge that we are unattractive to all potential mates if only a few of them have treated us as though we were unattractive. And memories formed during times of stress can be quite fallible and prone to inaccuracy (Jelinek et al. 2010).

Andy, however, faces a different problem where his experience is concerned. It's not that he is misremembering the many negative experiences with his mother; it's that they are driving his behavior when what he learned from them is least useful to him.

Andy is experiencing the downside of implicit learning. Throughout the course of his life, he has learned a lot about the way relationships work. Not surprisingly, all that learning leads to rules for operating in the world. A good mind will protect its owner in complex relationships, just as Andy's mind tries to protect him from angry women despite the fact that he no longer needs such protection. In complex relationships, the mind does a special variety of learning designed to keep relationships predictable and running smoothly—or if not smoothly, at least in a familiar manner. Using relationship history, the mind derives what some psychologists refer to as an *internal working model* (Bretherton and Munholland 1999).

Think of an internal working model as a learned advisor. It tells you not only where you've been in relationships, but how you should respond to a current situation based on what has worked best in the past. So, for example, if a child experiences a family that routinely condemns and criticizes sadness and tears, then as an adult that person will most likely come to expect condemnation and criticism for sadness in other important relationships.

There's an obvious adaptive value in knowing what to expect, but that's only half of the equation. The real value of internal working models comes when the mind starts repeating what it has heard from others. The child who was condemned and criticized for crying will one day come to condemn and criticize herself, often in a strikingly similar way. If her parents said, "Stop being a baby, you should be thankful for what you have," her mind is likely to give her something very similar later in life. *I'm being such a baby. I should be thankful for what I have.* She may never realize that she's telling herself the same things that others have told her; by chastising herself for sadness, she's applying her family's behavior to herself in their absence.

It's a brilliant survival strategy, and one that Andy no doubt applies when Meg is angry with him. If I were Andy's mind, I would tell him something like this: *I must have done something stupid and careless to make her so angry. I must stand still and keep my mouth shut so she doesn't become even angrier.* At the moment, he's so anxious that he doesn't realize how much his own mind sounds like his mother.

It's a brilliant strategy, though sometimes overgeneralized and self-defeating. Minds have great difficulty recognizing this simple fact: *that was then and this is now.* Andy knows that Meg is a very different person than his mother was, but his mind sees only danger when her anger appears, and it does what has worked in the past in order to protect him.

Psychologist Sarah Burgamy illustrates the mind's tendency to revive old behavior during times of stress (personal communication, February 17, 2011). Her metaphor involves shoes with laces, which you have probably been tying in a particular fashion for most of your life. By now, you can probably tie your shoes with your eyes closed, while engaged in conversation. The behavior is that practiced and automatic.

Imagine that Sarah teaches you a new way to tie your shoes. Perhaps it's a better or more efficient method. But because it's new, it requires more attention than your old method. You can no longer tie your shoes with your eyes closed. At least, not until you've had quite a bit of practice.

Now imagine that, as you are tying your shoes, a drill sergeant stands over you, shouting, "Tie your shoes, maggot! NOW!" Which method do you suppose your mind will turn to? The new, nuanced shoe-tying method or the trusty, old standby? Most minds will go with what they know.

Sometimes what we "know" about the world is inaccurate or incomplete. But minds aren't interested in nuanced wisdom. They're interested in saving us when times are tough. What better way to survive today's turmoil than turning to lessons already learned? Our minds hit us with fear and anxiety and compel us, sometimes against our will, to repeat responses that were once effective, even though those responses no longer serve us.

So why do we allow the mind to get away with it? Because acting on history is self-affirming. Each time Andy avoids an argument with his wife and survives, his mind chalks it up as a success. Each time Meg eventually calms down and *doesn't* call Andy stupid, his mind tallies one more piece of evidence that shutting down is an effective survival strategy.

Andy can gain insight into his own history, and he need not be ruled by it. The first step, as always, is observing the mind in action so that it cannot blindside us. Here's an exercise to help you learn how to do this.

Exercise: Questioning the "Facts" of Life

Having lived through our own histories, you would think, we should be experts on the matter. Most of us can recount the events of our lives with ease, but it takes special effort to understand how our minds use history to direct us, especially during challenging moments.

For this exercise, think of a recent difficult interaction—a disagreement with a loved one, a conflict with your boss, or a tense exchange with a stranger. See if you can observe your mind from a distance using the same practices we discussed in chapter 3: visualizing tiny soldiers on parade, using the phrase "I'm experiencing the thought," focusing outward when thoughts and feelings become overwhelming, and reminding yourself that thoughts and feelings are not facts

In particular, watch for thoughts and feelings that seem factual about yourself and about others. Be particularly mindful of thoughts containing the "always," "never," "should," and "must" sentiments:

* Men will never treat me right.

* Women will always take advantage of me.

* Coworkers always steal my work.

...And watch for judgments about your own reactions.

* I shouldn't be angry about this.

* I must look like a fool for being so emotional.

* No normal person would react this way.

Notice what your mind compels you to do in response to these "facts." For example, Andy falls silent when he feels that he's under attack. To his mind, it is a fact that he's better off remaining silent. Even if he wants to speak, he feels as if that is impossible, as if his mind is physically blocking him. What does your mind demand during difficult exchanges?

You might take notes over the course of several weeks to see if patterns emerge when you face difficult situations. What does your mind tell you to be true about the world, yourself, and relationships? Important bits of history probably underlie what your mind believes to be true. And after years of practicing behaviors based on your history, your mind has probably gotten very good at it.

Finally, when you can notice what your mind holds to be factual, and what it wants you to do in response to the "facts" of life, explore the opposites and the shades of gray. Remind yourself that what your mind holds to be absolutely true—based on history—may be true only some of the time. You probably won't persuade your mind to take a broader view of history, but you don't need to. Simply observing the mind creates options for you.

Why Our Minds Rely on History

The mind simply loves history, and what's not to love? The ability to gather and apply lessons from the environment is one of its primary jobs. We do it better than any other creature. In previous chapters, we've seen how the mind can take hold and direct us, and it can take hold of us when it believes we should repeat behaviors that have worked in the past—just ask Andy. There are two types of situations in particular when the mind insists that we obey the lessons of history.

The first is when problems arise, like when Andy's wife is angry with him. The advantage is that we can avoid new, untried responses that may backfire. We can go with what we know, and from a mind's point of view, that's almost always a safe bet. New behaviors come with unpredictable consequences, and they can exact a heavy cost if we guess poorly. Old behaviors are reliable, even if they are imperfect. That's good enough for a mind concerned with survival over happiness.

The second case in which the mind insists that we turn to history is during vague situations. Vague situations call for novel responses, and novel responses can be costly. Imagine walking into a church or temple of a religion you know nothing about. You don't know the rules or the expectations, but you know that breaking the rules might offend those around you.

Until you get your bearings, you can at least apply lessons learned in similar contexts—that is, in other religious institutions with which you are familiar. *Speak softly, be deferential, and try to imitate others*, your mind might insist. It may not be the perfect response, but it's better than trying something random like marching to the pulpit and demanding a beer. If you disobey your mind, you're likely to get an unpleasant dose of anxiety.

Staying Flexible When the Mind Is Stuck in the Past

The mind uses history in a way that furthers our survival. The tradeoff, as we've seen, is the loss of psychological flexibility. While Andy's response to an angry wife is effective in the most rudimentary sense, he misses out on any number of far more rewarding responses. Ironically, our minds' slavish adherence to history often creates the very problem that the mind is trying to avoid. Andy's withdrawal, for example, is meant to placate Meg. Instead, it only creates more anger. His mind is hoping to avoid a fight, and it gets a bigger one. Thanks, mind.

The Questioning the "Facts" of Life exercise above helps you understand when your mind insists that you repeat history. As you become more skilled at noticing your mind's adherence to the past, I suggest that you thank it for doing a superb job. Listen to it if you wish, and then choose your own best response. As you choose your own response, you increase your psychological flexibility.

A second way to increase psychological flexibility is to practice how you want to remember new events rather than allowing the mind to place new events into old, familiar schemes. Here's an exercise to help you choose how to remember new events.

Exercise: How Do I Want to Remember This?

That was then and this is now is a most difficult concept for survival-driven minds to grasp. It takes special effort on behalf of our higher minds to create a complete picture of our own history. Left to its own devices, the mind will remember events in a way that furthers survival rather than happiness or psychological flexibility. When the mind uses history to protect us, it often finds a way to make history repeat itself.

For this exercise, think back to another recent and troubling interaction in your life—an argument with a partner, a confrontation with a boss, a bad date, or a similar event. Next, see if you can notice your mind trying to categorize the experience.

For example, let's suppose you chose to recall a bad date. If you've had previous bad dating experiences (and who hasn't?), you may notice your mind categorizing it as one more piece of evidence that potential mates cannot be trusted. **No one can be trusted, and that jerk just proved it. Don't make the mistake of trusting anyone, ever again.** Yes, minds can be that strident.

The problem with allowing the mind to take us down that path without deliberately considering (not arguing) alternative viewpoints is that the mind will find ways to manifest what it believes to be true. If we buy into the "fact" that potential partners cannot be trusted, then we are unlikely to recognize trustworthy people. And if we do allow a trustworthy person to get close, they may very well be discouraged by our suspiciousness. **Voilà!** The mind has created a self-fulfilling prophecy.

A tried and true method for preventing the mind from proving itself right is to reflect on new experiences, especially painful ones, and decide how we want to remember them, while knowing full well that the mind will keep its own survival-driven version. After a bad experience like the hypothetical blind date, it can be useful to ask these questions of ourselves:

* How do I want to remember this experience?

* What is the most useful thing to remember about it?

* Does this experience feel familiar to me? Have I experienced something similar?

* What factors contributed to this experience?

* What factors were within my control, and what lay outside my control?

One of the most useful things we can do following a difficult experience is to simply write about it. Engaging in a systematic, written analysis of painful events improves well-being in a way that merely thinking about it does not (Lyubomirsky, Sousa, and Dickerhoof 2006). The goal of writing about bad experiences is not to persuade yourself to take a certain viewpoint, to vent, or to convince your mind that it wasn't painful, but simply to balance the scales of evidence and develop a complete and coherent account rather than the simplistic and self-protective account to which the mind will default.

If you choose to write about a painful event, you might begin by simply recording the events as you remember them, along with your reactions. Then you might use the questions above to help you paint a complete and coherent picture of the events so that your recall is colored by thoughtful detachment. When the mind says, **This date is being quiet and obviously doesn't want to be with me**, the **facts** are that people can behave quietly for any number of reasons. Perhaps they're not feeling well, or their cat just died, or they're overcome by their attraction to you. When the mind insists that old patterns are repeating, it may be time to investigate the facts.

In our rational minds, we make distinctions about events in our history. We're capable of recognizing that *that was then and this is now*. Our primitive minds, on the other hand, may try to convince us that *that was then, and this is then*. By piling on the emotion, it tries to coerce us into acting as if we are facing old dangers even when we're safe.

In the next chapter, we will examine another coercive trick of the mind that can feel every bit as compelling, and equally laden with emotion.

Chapter 8

Trump Cards and Double Standards

E ven as a trained psychologist, I am sometimes unwittingly drawn into
arguing with a client's mind. One man in particular was cornered by
the thoughts that his marriage, his job, and his life were hopeless, and
that he was an utter mess of a human being. At every example and explanation of just how broken and hopeless he was, I would dutifully counter with a
well-crafted rejoinder. I wanted to convince him that he had built a good life
for himself, and I cited one example after another of how smart, capable, and
important he was.

After several minutes of this well-intentioned bickering, he sighed, looked
me in the eye, and said, "I know all that, but I still suck."

All of my arguments had been trumped. How could I refute a thought so
laden with emotion and determination? I realized that I had been drawn into
an argument that I could not possibly win.

Sometimes the mind simply cannot be outmaneuvered, either because it
is technically correct (like when it says that *this* could be the time that the
airplane crashes) or because it is simply being relentless and uncompromising.
For my client, the thought *I still suck* was his mind's way of insisting that the
solutions to his problems lay somewhere within himself. His life would
improve if only he could "suck" less. Or so his mind seemed to believe, and
my client was buying into that thought.

I was also unintentionally buying into the thought, in a different way. I was hooked on the idea that the thought was so important that it had to be refuted.

These are the kinds of thoughts that hit us when we least want them, and when we are most vulnerable to them. They hit us when we're depressed, defeated, or trying desperately to get ourselves moving in the right direction. They seem designed to keep us down. They materialize like gremlins during our most challenging moments. I'm talking about thoughts that cut deep, like *If they really knew me, they would see what a fraud I am,* or *This could be the time that everything falls apart forever,* or *It doesn't matter what they say, I'm still damaged goods.*

What's worse, we often lack enough ammunition to defeat these kinds of thoughts. They seem irrefutable because, thanks to the old file drawer problem, the times when things didn't go that way don't get "published" in our minds. Perhaps their seeming irrefutability is precisely their purpose. From a mind's point of view, what good is all that history-gathering if it cannot be used to keep us on the safest path?

To keep us on that safe path, the mind seems to require the ability to stop us cold, whether it's through panic, a freeze response, or, on a more sophisticated level, thoughts that discourage us from risk. That last item—thoughts that immobilize us—are the topic of this chapter. These are the mind's trump cards and double standards.

Trump Cards

Safety and survival seem to be the driving forces behind our most painful thoughts and feelings. The mind doesn't use trump-card arguments merely to torment us. It has no interest in such sport, as far as I know. The mind gives us irrefutable thoughts in the service of safety. The survival-driven worry machine will always fight for our safety, even if it must immobilize us to do so.

In chapter 1, we looked at a few examples of what many psychologists refer to as irrational thoughts. With sufficient effort, we can sometimes out-maneuver cognitive sand traps such as all-or-none thinking, catastrophizing, focusing on the negative, or personalization. But trump-card thoughts are different. They are not sand traps; they are quicksand. These very persuasive thoughts can feel as factual as the sun in the sky.

What makes these thoughts so difficult to refute? First, they are laden with emotion. As we have seen, emotion tends to add the illusion of factualness. More importantly, these thoughts tend to be based on experience—selective experience, as the mind is prone to gathering—and experience is a difficult thing to dispute.

Lest you think that you are alone if you notice these thoughts from your own mind, rest easy. I have yet to meet a mind that does not invoke some form of trump-card thoughts when it is wrestling with a difficult problem. These are some of the most common:

* *If you really knew me...*

* *Yes, but I'm still broken.*

* *This could be the time that it all falls apart.*

* *But what about the time...*

As you can probably guess by now, I'm going to suggest that one response to these intransigent thoughts is accepting them for what they are rather than arguing with them. That is not to suggest that you should believe these thoughts, but simply that trying to refute them may be exhausting and unproductive.

Perhaps these thoughts are not the enemy. Perhaps they even exist to serve us. You might think of these thoughts as a kind of neurotic Justice League—that is, superheros who are able to bring things to a grinding halt before we get hurt.

Your mind may come up with its own unique thoughts, different from those in the list above, that leave you stumped and frozen. The form of the particular thought matters less than the function. Let's deconstruct these few examples, and then we will discuss how to respond to the mind's trump-card arguments, whatever their form.

If You Really Knew Me...

Imagine you have just met your significant other's family for the first time. You were nervous for days prior, but despite your anxiety the family seemed to love you. They greeted you warmly, appeared genuinely interested in you, and laughed at your jokes. They even invited you to their next family gathering and asked you to bring your special potato salad they've heard so much about.

Despite all that, you had difficulty believing that they truly enjoyed you. You find one reason after another to doubt their sincerity. Uncle Joe was only being polite; Aunt Margaret seems phony; Cousin Mike was obviously buttering you up for a favor. Thoughts like these may be especially strong if you have a history of undependable relationships. Your mind simply isn't willing to trust that they have truly embraced you. It fears their rejection.

Finally, when your significant other tries to reassure you that they did indeed find you charming and likeable, a little voice pipes up like a gremlin from the past: *But if they really knew me, they wouldn't want me to date you.*

Facts and evidence be damned, the mind has just played a trump card. Each time I have encountered this type of relentless thinking, it has existed in the service of a fairly obvious and important goal: to avoid rejection. *If they really knew me...* is the mind's way of keeping you on your best behavior in the presence of important people so that you don't disappoint them and earn their scorn.

This thought comes with a dangerous trap. Trying to suppress it prompts the mind to recall specific examples in support of the notion that you are hiding deep flaws. *Remember the time you were fired? That proves what a loser you are. Remember the time you were dumped? Don't let them find out that you're damaged goods.* The mind can always find one more piece of evidence.

That process is precisely what happened when I argued with my client until he eventually told me, "I still suck." By arguing, I only encouraged his mind to contrive evidence until he drew the inevitable (and wrong) conclusion.

The other danger with this type of thought is the paradoxical effect that follows if we buy into it. Believing this thought can ultimately help you lose the very thing that the mind hopes to protect.

If you buy into this thought, either by believing it or getting caught up in trying to disprove it, you may find yourself acting as if it were true. When Aunt Margaret asks you to bring your famous potato salad to the next gathering and you demur, she's likely to sense your mind's defensiveness. Your own mind may create strained, distant interactions as it tries to prevent her from truly getting to know you. Eventually, she will sense that you're rejecting her advances and she will withdraw, confirming your original suspicions. What begins as the mind's attempt to avoid rejection can ironically invite rejection. The mind has an uncanny way of manifesting its own fears.

So how should we respond when fighting a thought might strengthen it and believing it might be disastrous? A third path may be the safest: allow the thought to exist and resist the temptation to believe that it is either right or wrong. Don't get drawn into a game of chess. Instead, recognize the thought for what it is—the mind's urgent need to protect you from rejection.

It takes practice, and it's normal to struggle with distancing ourselves from the chess game, especially when we have spent a lifetime believing some of our thoughts. But even after a lifetime's worth of investment in a thought, it is still just a thought.

Yes, But I'm Still Broken

Oddly enough, a thought like this tends to come around when things are going relatively well, and often when we are recovering from a loss. For example, a person may be developing a close romantic relationship after a string of painful breakups. Just as she begins to experience the trust and bonding of her new relationship, her mind begins to worry: *This may feel like an ideal relationship, but remember: I'm still broken.*

This thought can feel as if the mind is tormenting us for the pure sport of it. But more likely, this is the mind's attempt to reconcile unsolved problems, and more importantly, to prevent them from happening again. You might recall Luke's dilemma from chapter 1. His mind desperately wanted to prevent old patterns from repeating in a new relationship. If he could figure out what he had been doing wrong in previous relationships, his mind seemed to think, he might be able to prevent a recurrence. *I'm still broken* is the mind's attempt to avoid dangerous complacency and to repair old patterns.

Like the previous thought, *if you really knew me,* arguing with this one is risky business. The mind will have no trouble selectively sifting through history to make its point. And like the previous thought, buying into this one can lead us to do things that make the thought come true, as it did with Luke.

Once again, the third path may be the most useful and productive. Recognize the protective nature of the thought, thank your mind for it, and step away from the chess match.

This Could Be the Time That It All Falls Apart

Thank goodness for these minds, always on duty avoiding danger and complacency. This thought is pessimism writ large, and it exists for our safety. It is designed to keep us from making what might be a costly mistake. (This thought gives us a preview of pessimistic thinking, which we will discuss more fully, especially its protective features, in the next chapter.)

Like other trump cards, the mind plays this one at the most relevant (and least convenient) times. When you would most prefer to enjoy confidence and steady nerves, your mind may just give you the opposite experience.

This thought is likeliest to arise in a situation that will *probably* be okay, but has the potential to work out poorly. Air travel is a good example. While it's remarkably safe, the mind is likely to remind you that this could be the time that things go horribly wrong.

The particular difficulty with this thought is that it is technically correct. Each and every flight *could* be the one that crashes. It's unlikely, but possible. If you argue with the mind, explaining that virtually every other airliner has landed safely, it's likely to tell you that it doesn't care about the other airplanes—it cares about *this* one. And it's going to make sure that you feel appropriately anxious.

This trump card is grounded in a rather simple bit of survival logic: it is better to guess that a situation is dangerous and be wrong than to mistakenly assume the situation is safe. Chapters 5 and 6 offered skills for responding to an anxious mind with compassion and acceptance, and, as I mentioned above, we will return to the topic of pessimism in the next chapter.

But What About the Time...

Speaking of anxious minds, this is another thought designed to immobilize us and keep us safe, and it tends to arise when we least want it. *But what about the time...* is a manifestation of that all-powerful one-trial learning. Remember Andy's overgeneralized reaction to angry women? The mind *hates* making the same mistake twice.

The unique difficulty behind this thought is that it is often hard to spot. Perhaps that's because this thought is typically accompanied by enough anxiety to cloud our mental functioning, and perhaps because its root is sometimes difficult to pinpoint.

Imagine a young woman who was once utterly humiliated while on a bad date. Years later, while on a date with a man who somehow reminds her of the cad who mistreated her, she finds herself feeling anxious and behaving rudely. She may not realize that her mind has noticed some similarity between the two men and has given her a jolt of anxiety and anger to protect her from repeating the earlier experience. Both of them leave the date wondering what happened.

By ruining what might have turned out to be a wonderful date, the mind has done its job of protecting her; the irony is that it has created one more bad dating experience to use as evidence in the future. The next time she prepares for a date, her mind may start shouting, *but what about the time....* She may not realize what's happening as she begins to experience the old anxiety and anger. This is why it is so vital to keep an eye on the mind and understand what it is trying to accomplish.

Responding to Trump Cards

This is not a complete list of the mind's trump-card arguments. You may have discovered your own. One of my personal favorites, and a quite common one, is *This one is a fluke.* This thought functions to keep us from becoming too invested in something that we believe we don't deserve or that could go away at any moment, be it a job, a relationship, or a financial gain. This thought reins in our enthusiasm and restricts our behavior. Of course, by distracting and distancing us from our good fortune, the mind only increases the odds of actually losing what we desperately hope to maintain.

That's the irony of the mind's trump cards. A skydiving instructor once cautioned me to avoid looking at oil rigs and power lines on my way down. If you stare at them, he said, you're likely to hit them. He knew that I might focus on those hazards in the service of avoiding them, but doing so might have the unfortunate, paradoxical effect of crashing into them.

The mind's trump-card thoughts function similarly. When we give them prominence, either by believing them or by fighting against them, we increase the odds of achieving precisely what the mind hopes to avoid.

These thoughts are some of the mind's most persuasive tools. *Do not ignore me! I won't let you,* it seems to say. We *can* ignore thoughts if we remember to notice and appreciate what the mind is up to. It doesn't come naturally because they're designed to keep us safe. You may not even notice that your mind has invoked a trump card until later, but each time you recognize what happened, it becomes easier to notice it the next time it happens. Bottom line: It is somewhat unnatural, and it takes practice. Be patient with yourself. Use these four strategies for responding to the mind's most stubborn arguments: check the facts, cultivate a coherent view of your history, consider explanations not naturally offered by your mind, and know when your mind cannot be trusted. Let's take a closer look at each of these strategies now.

1. Check the Facts

Your mind might be saying that you're entering the gates of hell, but what does the environment say? Are you in physical danger? Are you at risk of losing relationships? Is there any dangerous problem at hand? If the answer is no, then perhaps it's best to ignore the mind. There's no need to argue with your mind about the facts. Instead, allow yourself to have two sets of thoughts at one time—those thoughts and feelings that you don't choose as well as the thoughts on objective observations. If you're anxious as you prepare to give a speech, for example, perhaps you can allow the anxiety to exist alongside an objective appraisal of the situation. Like pieces on the metaphorical chessboard, there is no need to eliminate one side or the other. You have only to decide how you will act.

2. Cultivate a Coherent View of Your History

Recognize that the mind is biased toward remembering dangerous events. It's the old file drawer problem. Take special effort to recall *all* of your history—warts and halos alike. The How Do I Want to Remember This? exercise at the end of the previous chapter offers pointers for battling the file drawer problem. You can apply that exercise to recent events as well as events of long ago.

3. Consider Explanations Not Naturally Offered by Your Mind

As we've already discovered, most minds seek self-critical explanations when no other is forthcoming. (Alternatively, some minds consistently place blame on other people or outside circumstances, which can be equally self-defeating.) Your mind may tell you, for example, that Aunt Margaret was distant at the last family gathering because she is angry with you. But perhaps her actions have nothing to do with you. The old adage is often true: people don't think about us nearly as much as we imagine.

Finding alternative explanations does not come naturally. It's much easier to allow the mind to arrive at its usual explanations. But finding alternatives is a relatively straightforward task that involves identifying factors, other than you, that might have affected the situation. Maybe Aunt Margaret was in an argument with Uncle Joe. Maybe she's not feeling well. Maybe she's having difficulty at work.

Above all, don't be afraid to check the facts. If Aunt Margaret is acting odd, ask her what's up. The mind does its worst to us when we allow ourselves to become isolated with our thoughts.

4. Know When Your Mind Cannot Be Trusted

For all of us, there are times and situations in which the mind is simply not to be trusted, such as when we are fatigued or frustrated by unrelated influences. We're more likely to argue about little problems at home, for example, when our minds are worried about problems at work. Being able to identify when we are most vulnerable to the mind's messages is a remarkably liberating skill.

That involves stepping away from small situations and examining larger trends. Am I sleep deprived? Hungry? Angry at my boss? We'll be returning to the topics of mood and self-care in part 4, where we'll discuss in some detail how to defend ourselves against troubling states of mind.

Double Standards

Healthy minds have two sets of standards: one for everyone else, and one for themselves. A highly motivated student may be terribly self-critical for receiving a grade of B in a difficult class, while at the same time recognizing that a B is perfectly acceptable—for someone else, that is.

Such double standards are painful when they force us to experience something we hope to avoid. The high-achieving, self-critical student can find that grade of B to be excruciating if it reminds him that he cannot always control outcomes, or worse, if he fears it will trigger disappointment in people important to him.

Why would a healthy mind put us through such a thing? Connection to others is all-important to the mind, and the type of double standards we discuss in this chapter are intertwined with that basic survival drive. A good mind will be hypersensitive to the possibility of abandonment, and so it ups its chances of remaining connected by setting unforgiving standards for the self and more relaxed standards for others.

Consider, for example, a situation that most parents have experienced. Imagine taking your toddler to the grocery store, or the playground, or some other crowded venue, when you notice that your child is nowhere in sight. Panic sets in, but soon enough the child turns up. Very few of us will think to ourselves, *Eh, don't worry about it, it happens to everyone.*

That is precisely what most of us would say to another parent, but most of us who have been in the position are far less forgiving of ourselves. *You idiot! You're a terrible parent! Keep track of your kid next time!*

In 1954, Leon Festinger published one of psychology's more famous papers, in which he noted that comparing ourselves to others is a staple of human social activity. He proposed that we have a powerful drive to evaluate ourselves, and that we rely on others similar to us as a basis of comparison. Mothers compare themselves to other mothers, students to other students, and psychologists to other psychologists.

Since Festinger published his paper, there have been numerous theories and mountains of research on the ways in which we compare ourselves to others. Mating, advancement, opinion forming, jealousy, justice, and performance are a few of the human concerns that researchers have tied to social comparison. We won't try to sort out any of those ponderous topics, but we will examine double standards as they affect us in the moment.

Double standards, which would not exist without the drive to compare ourselves to others, seem to function at least in part as a kind of social insurance. Holding ourselves to a higher standard than others provides a margin of safety. The downside is that they are painful and, like the mind's trump cards, can help us achieve what we least desire.

Performance Double Standards

Being the irrepressibly social creatures that we are, we need to stay in the good graces of others. One of the most basic ways to accomplish this is to be competent and useful. Double standards concerning our performance help us stay on top of our game—as long as they don't consume us and create a paradoxical effect.

Consider the mother who scolds herself harshly for losing track of her toddler when she would have been perfectly forgiving of that honest mistake in someone else. The immediate function of that double standard seems fairly obvious. It calls her attention to the fact that she made a mistake and forces her to reflect on it, thereby decreasing the chances that she will do it again. That is sound survival logic, and no small benefit to her kin. In other words, it's useful.

This double standard loses its utility when her self-criticism becomes so engrossing that it begins to interfere with good parenting. She may, for example, become so protective of her child that she denies him the freedom to explore, make mistakes, and become a resourceful person (all the while granting other parents her patience and tolerance). The paradox of such a desperate desire to protect her child is that she may ultimately harm him by denying him the opportunity to learn from his own mistakes.

The mind, in its dogged pursuit of safety, sometimes seems incapable of predicting unintended consequences.

Historical Double Standards

This example is perhaps not a double standard so much as a cognitive bias, and it works like this: when I think about you, I recall the good and the bad; when I think of myself, I tend to recall my most painful and embarrassing moments.

As we have discussed elsewhere, the purpose of such a bias is to prevent us from repeating mistakes, but it obviously becomes a detriment when it clouds our judgment about ourselves.

A friend of mine was once considered for a supervisory position but was skeptical about her ability to perform the job. When she thought about her job performance up to that point, she could recall only her mistakes and lapses in judgment. Because of her self-doubt, she declined the promotion and the job went to someone she believed to be quite capable but who was, by all accounts, far less qualified.

The bias to remember our mistakes, while glossing over the mistakes of others, offers a fairly obvious survival advantage. It keeps us from repeating errors. It also helps us recognize our limits and avoid getting in over our head, which was my friend's fear.

But taken too far, it can prevent us from holding a realistic and coherent view of ourselves. My friend's double standard about performance was intended to protect her and the organization. In the end, both suffered because of it.

Emotional Double Standards

Stoicism is a wonderful human quality, up to a point. Most of us, at least where I come from, want to keep our emotions in check, lest they lead us down a destructive path. We prefer to keep a stiff upper lip, as the British say.

We tend to be fairly forgiving of the emotions of others. We expect others to cry at weddings and funerals, and we allow "mental health days" for our coworkers who are feeling overwhelmed. But very few of us want to be the one who is crying at the funeral (how many times have you heard someone say, "I told myself I wasn't going to cry!"). And when it comes to the more over-whelming emotions—the kind that might lead to a mental health day—we tend to believe that our own emotions are inappropriate. I'm *too* happy, *too* sad, *too* angry. I've lost track of the number of clients who have told me, "I have no right to feel this way," when it seemed to me that their emotions were perfectly appropriate.

We tend to judge our emotions particularly harshly when we notice that there are other people in the world who are suffering. "I have no right to feel this way when there is so much suffering in the world." If we followed that logic to its conclusion, then only one person at a time (the person who was having the worst day in the world) would be allowed to feel upset. Everyone else would have to count their good fortune, no matter how bad their predicament.

We have very little control over our emotions, and we have already discussed the pitfalls of trying to prevent them. This double standard can drag us down that road without our awareness, if we fail to recognize it.

Responding to Double Standards

To paraphrase the writer G. K. Chesterton, behind every double standard lies a single agenda. In this case, that agenda seems to be the mind's constant concern that we avoid mistakes, especially costly social mistakes. They force us to keep our own behavior up to snuff and motivate us to forgive others. These are both good survival strategies.

The key to responding to these natural and healthy tendencies, I think, is to simply observe them as they are happening, understand their purpose, and choose our own course of action when they are having an unproductive, paradoxical effect. There is no need to eliminate them; we can proceed in spite of them.

Sometimes that requires questioning our self-judgments, which can be quite uncomfortable. Because our self-evaluations are intertwined with the mind's survival logic, questioning them can feel like we're flirting with social disaster. Luckily, we humans can handle a bit of discomfort in the service of making reasonable judgments about ourselves.

In order to prevent our otherwise healthy double standards from going too far and becoming detrimental, it's vital to be able to distinguish between facts and emotional evaluations.

For example, someone being considered for a promotion might have thoughts like *I've handled contracts poorly, I don't do well with subordinates, and I probably can't handle the added responsibility.* Those are judgments, not facts. Facts look like this: *I correctly managed 93 percent of my contracts and made identifiable mistakes on 7 percent, ten out of twelve peers rated me positively at my last review, and I will need to improve my time-management skills in order to handle the added responsibility.*

Those two evaluations of the same situation paint very different pictures. In the exercise below, I invite you to examine the evaluations you make in your own life.

Exercise: Judgments and Facts

We've outlined above three common areas where minds tend to invoke double standards: performance, history, and emotions. Now I'd like you to recall a time when you applied a double standard to yourself. It probably won't be difficult to find one. Think back to any situation in which your mind gave you some of the thoughts we discussed above, such as beating up on yourself for something you find forgivable in others, judging yourself as being odd in comparison to others, or experiencing thoughts such as **I'm too upset about this**.

Once you have identified a double standard, bring it into the light by writing a paragraph on each of these three topics:

* Topic 1: What my mind says about my performance, history, emotions, and so on.

* Topic 2: What I expect of myself

* Topic 3: What I expect of others

By the time you finish, you should have a clear view of what your mind is up to and what it might be trying to accomplish. For example, you might notice that your mind is trying to ensure that your job performance exceeds expectations in order to maintain job security. Perhaps you'll decide that your mind is being harsh to the point of detriment. If so, you can notice that thought and carry it with you as you go forward. On the other hand, you may decide that you wish to abide by your mind's double standard. The choice is yours. There is no wrong answer; there is nothing inherently wrong with double standards. The challenge, as always, is to follow your values with full awareness rather than being dragged along by a vague dictate from the mind.

Staying Observant and Maintaining Distance

Trump cards and double standards are part of the mind's survival logic. They exist for a reason, and sometimes they're right. When the mind says, *Don't ignore me! I won't let you!*, it may be trying to tell you something important. The key to knowing whether or not to trust the mind lies in the ability to discern fact from emotion-based evaluation.

That skill requires the ability to observe the mind from a distance so that we can avoid being drawn into a costly battle against our own inner workings. Hopefully by now you have had the chance to practice some of the observing and distancing skills that we have discussed, such as the Tiny Soldiers on Parade exercise, the I Am Experiencing the Thought exercise, and the racetrack metaphor (see chapter 3). In particular, it helps to remember what the mind is trying to achieve. By now, you may be noticing your mind worrying about safety and survival when the concerns at hand pose no real threat. It is odd indeed that the mind can get caught up in the business of saving our lives when all we really need to do is navigate fairly mundane situations like a first date or a disagreement with the boss.

A quick reality check might also help establish some distance from the mind. For example, you might notice your body reacting *as if* you were in physical danger as you prepare for public speaking—increased heart rate, rapid breathing, sweating, and so on. Since we know that arguing with the mind in cases like that can sometimes make the problem worse, you might simply thank your mind for watching out for you, remind yourself that your mind does not have all the facts, and move forward in the service of your values. We need not prove our minds wrong in order to go on with the business of life.

Chapter 9

Pessimistic Thinking

With selective recall of history, trump cards, and double standards, the mind can be awfully persuasive. This next human characteristic, pessimistic thinking, can be just as persuasive, and like the others, it can be a real downer.

Not only is it normal to experience pessimistic thoughts, but it is also normal to experience judgment from others and social pressure to avoid negative thinking. When we confess to pessimistic thoughts, we're likely to hear remarks such as "Stay positive" or "You shouldn't think that way."

I prefer to be more optimistic about pessimism. Just like the other thought processes we've discussed, pessimism appears to have strong survival value. It might exist for the very basic purpose of saving our lives, and it can be very insistent in the pursuit of that goal.

Pessimistic thinking—the tendency to see the flaws in situations and to anticipate undesirable outcomes—is ubiquitous among human minds. That is not to suggest that all of us tend toward pessimism. Some don't. Of those whose minds are more pessimistic, some have more success with it than others. We will discuss why in a bit.

The mind can be the ultimate naysayer. *This won't work. That is imperfect. This plan will backfire.* One of my most influential instructors, psychologist Ragnar Storaasli, illustrates the universal experience of pessimism with a telling metaphor (personal communication, November 5, 2010).

Imagine walking down a street in a foreign city when you pass a cathedral with beautiful stained-glass windows. The designs are intricate, the colors are brilliant, and the craftsmanship is exquisite. There is just one problem. One of the windows has a missing piece of glass. Where do you think most normal minds will want to focus?

I can tell you that my mind would fixate on the flaw. *What a shame, that stain on such a beautiful piece of art. Cold air must be rushing into the cathedral, and that missing glass is an open invitation for pests!* There is little chance that I would miss the flaw, and having noticed it, it would take conscious effort in order to enjoy the artwork while my mind fixated on that niggling little imperfection. It seems that we are simply wired to notice problems. One has to wonder what necessitates such torment.

The issue seems to be not so much that we are wired for negative evaluations, but that the mind is programmed to calculate probabilities and manage errors. The mind understands that we will make mistakes as we move about in the environment, and that some mistakes aren't as risky as others.

The mind seems to be brilliant at hypothesis testing. Imagine an ancient hunter moving about in the underbrush when he hears a rustling in a nearby bush. He knows that there are other predators in the area, and he can act on one of two possibilities. Either he bets that there is something dangerous behind the bush and he retreats, or he wagers that there is no danger and happily returns to his hunting.

Either possibility could be wrong, but the latter one comes with a much higher cost, and the mind knows it. This is the beauty of pessimism. The mind would rather make a false-positive error (detecting a problem that doesn't exist) than a false-negative error (failing to detect a problem that *does* exist). The mind is prone to detect danger even when danger is unlikely to exist, because in a world where errors are a given, making the right kind of errors increases the odds of survival (Haselton, Nettle, and Andrews 2005).

The result of this style of hypothesis testing is that our minds are perfectly willing to make mistakes, as long as they are the right kind of mistakes.

The downside to this brilliant survival mechanism is that it sometimes interferes with our ability to relax and enjoy the beauty around us. Our minds instantly and automatically draw our attention to the flaw in the stained-glass window, and perhaps that's why we judge pessimism so harshly. Not me. I'm optimistic about pessimism.

It Isn't Pessimism—It's Error Management

It often pays to err on the side of pessimism. Aversion to strangers, for example, is a universal human experience that makes sense. If you assume that the neighboring clan is dangerous and you turn out to be wrong, then there is no immediate cost. However, mistakenly betting that they are friendly and trustworthy could be fatal.

There are more mundane examples as well. Returning to the topic of trump cards for a moment, *They're just saying that* is a remarkably effective and persuasive one. When we doubt that we are in the good graces of others, those others may try to reassure us: "No, seriously, we're not upset with you. We think you're a wonderful person, and we want you in our lives." *They're just saying that,* responds the mind. It's better, from a mind's point of view, to assume they're falsely reassuring us and to remain appropriately contrite.

But it's not as if the mind sees danger around every corner. In some matters, the mind wagers in a more optimistic direction. Martie Haselton and colleagues (2005), for example, noticed that we tend to overestimate sexual interest from others. Men are particularly prone to this miscalculation, which may not be an error at all, because it happens to advance the survival of our species.

This is another of the mind's logical wagers. If a man bets that a woman is interested, he will pursue her. The worst likely outcome is rejection, in which case he really hasn't lost anything; the best possible outcome is a joyous and fruitful coupling. However, if he bets that she is uninterested, he will ignore her and therefore have no chance of mating. Better he should err on the optimistic side. This may explain why the lounge lizard at your local pub simply cannot get it through his head that the waitress is not interested.

These seemingly contradictory biases (pessimistic about reassurance; optimistic about sex) suggest that the mind is programmed to make the right kinds of errors in life rather than to avoid errors outright. For a mind limited in its ability to make accurate snap decisions in an uncertain world, probabilities are the next best thing to information. "Pessimism" and "optimism" are simply the value judgments that we place on the mind's inner workings.

And we do judge pessimism harshly, but not entirely without cause. Conventional wisdom, and a good bit of research, suggests that pessimism is associated with depression, inertia, poor physical health, and self-fulfilling prophecy (Seligman 2006). Perhaps that's why a rudimentary search at any large bookseller will yield dozens, if not hundreds, of titles on how to cultivate optimistic thinking.

Lest I leave you with the impression that I oppose cultivating positive thoughts and striving toward a happy mindset, I am very much in favor of these things. Because of our innate ability to spot problems, developing those skills requires practice but is most certainly worth the effort. After all, the entire thesis of this book is that we need not be imprisoned by our own minds. We can set ourselves free from our own insistent, oppressive thoughts.

The danger here is one of false dichotomy. Cultivating positive thoughts is one thing; trying to eradicate negative thoughts is another matter. Why not have both? Our minds have more than enough room to hold two sets of thoughts, and we have the capacity to decide which thoughts we wish to buy into and act upon.

We can spend our lives trying to eliminate negative thoughts, but perhaps there are better uses of our limited time. Besides, a "negative" thought is really just a thought upon which we have placed a value judgment. If I notice a flaw in a stained-glass window, for example, I can scold myself for fixating on it, or I can avoid the internal game of chess and view the thought for what it is: an inheritance from my ancestors giving me the ability to calculate probabilities and avoid problems. Thank you, ancestors, and thank you, mind!

Rather than asking how to eradicate such thoughts, perhaps the more useful questions at hand are these: How do we "do" pessimism in a most excellent fashion? How do we find the positive side of negative thinking?

Pessimism: The Ancient Cure for Modern Times

Pessimism does more than help us avoid danger and find flaws in stained-glass windows. It helps to solve problems. As psychologist Robert Leahy (2002) pointed out, much of our evolutionary history was lived on the edge of survival, and miscalculations could prove fatal.

Pessimism is an evolved thought process, shaped by our experience and designed to influence our future (hopefully for the positive). Its workings can be rather intricate. Leahy points out, for example, that pessimistic thinking can slow us down when we're moving too fast for our own good. Pessimism and self-criticism are part of what he calls a *behavioral inhibition system*. They contribute to a stop-loss process that minimizes the chances that we will repeat behaviors that previously have had bad payoffs.

Leahy explains that *anticipatory pessimism*, which takes the form of worry and hopelessness, slows us down and gives us a chance to think. By adding a bit of deliberation to our behavior, pessimism may have curbed our ancestors from returning to the same dry watering hole, and it keeps us from throwing good money after bad—figuratively or literally.

Pessimistic thinking also helps us anticipate likely problems, according to Leahy. Because our pessimistic nature points out flaws in the environment, we have the opportunity to devise solutions, or simply to sidestep oncoming difficulties.

The next time someone scolds you for a pessimistic thought, you might help them see the survival advantage in this mental armament. If you're feeling feisty, you might even point out the irony in holding such a pessimistic view of pessimism.

Still, pessimism can be as detrimental as anything else done poorly or to excess. Even with pessimism, technique matters.

Pessimism Done Right

Things have improved dramatically since our forefathers were hunting with spears. We've progressed from dodging predators to dodging traffic, which is generally more predictable. Basic needs are easily met for most of us in the Western world. We live in absolute luxury compared to even recent generations, to say nothing of distant ancestors who eked their daily living off the land. Perhaps unsurprisingly, we remain wired to detect problems despite our ideal living conditions—which may be part of the reason we continue to enjoy ideal living conditions.

Pessimism remains a wonderful problem-solving strategy if it is used correctly. A specific type, *defensive pessimism,* is an example of pessimism used to advantage. When faced with a difficult task or uncontrolled circumstances, the defensive pessimist will set low expectations and identify the things that might go wrong. Once they've identified the potential problems, they begin the crucial step of devising contingency plans (Norem 2008). A nervous real estate agent, for example, might explore all the ways in which a sale could go wrong, and then decide how she will respond to problems such as the most likely objections from the buyer, the most likely difficulties with the lender, and any other snares she can foresee.

Defensive pessimism might be another name for productive worrying. This pessimistic approach puts the real estate agent in an advantageous position. She has dramatically reduced her chances of being surprised by a problem. Equally important, her mental preparation can ease her anxiety, make the possibility of failure more tolerable, and give her a sense of control. Defensive pessimism has the dual functions of managing outcomes and managing anxiety.

Pessimism frequently gets a bad rap as being a self-fulfilling mind-set: "Don't think that way, or you'll make it come true." Perhaps that fear (which is deliciously pessimistic) is based on the experience that our minds can indeed drag us into a pit of hopelessness to the point that we become immobilized.

Interestingly, this superstitious line of thinking may be yet another of the mind's error-management techniques. The thinking goes something like this: *If I can banish negative thoughts, then they won't come true.* Just like any other pessimism-driven probability calculation, this superstitious thought makes sense from a certain point of view. There is little cost to believing that we can control outcomes by managing our minds, and there is theoretically much to gain (Haselton, Nettle, and Andrews 2005). In other words, this superstition doesn't cost anything. It may actually appear to pay off when we successfully banish pessimistic thoughts and things correspondingly work out well.

On the other hand, defensive pessimism is far from self-fulfilling. It can actually improve a person's performance, and it is a favorite strategy of many high achievers (Lim 2009).

Defensive pessimists perform similarly to people with a naturally optimistic approach, and they outperform *dispositional pessimists*—those who consistently expect negative outcomes but don't plan contingency responses or influence the outcome of a situation (del Valle and Mateos 2008). Instead of increased ability to respond to difficulties, dispositional pessimists tend to experience an increasing sense of helplessness.

Obviously, there are times when pessimism is detrimental, especially when a person becomes immobilized by depressing or fearful thoughts. But pessimism can be our friend. The magic ingredient appears to be *reflectivity*, which refers to the planning and strategizing that follows a pessimistic forecast. Reflectivity counteracts the immobilizing effects of pessimism by strengthening four factors related to performance:

* **Goal importance:** Defensive pessimists tend to set and pursue goals in order to avoid failure.

* **Effort:** Because defensive pessimists focus on avoiding negative outcomes, they tend to try harder.

* **Expectations:** Defensive pessimists become increasingly confident that they will succeed as they plan for their performance. Oddly enough, the fear of poor performance can actually increase confidence, as long as that fear is accompanied by planning.

* **Anticipated emotional recovery:** Because they anticipate the possibility of poor performance, defensive pessimists also anticipate that they will recover quickly from failure (Gasper, Lozinski, and LeBeau 2009). That speeds their recovery after a downfall. Like a resilient child who scrapes his knee, we tend to bounce back more quickly from problems when we possess the confidence that we will be able to tolerate them.

None of this is intended to give optimism short shrift, but simply to acknowledge and accept that some minds are more anxious and pessimistic than others. Clearly, optimistic thoughts can be useful. When a player's team is losing, it is the optimistic players who try harder to win (Gordon 2008). While we can certainly cultivate positive thoughts, it is difficult to transform an anxious, pessimistic mind into a pure optimist. That may be particularly true when the mind feels that it *should* be anxious, and that it *should* rely on this ancient, effective problem-solving strategy.

Living with a Pessimistic Mind

In light of our species' long and tested history of pessimistic thinking, whether or not we experience negative thoughts seems a settled question. For most of us, the thoughts will appear whether or not we like them. How we respond to those thoughts seems the more important issue. There are three strategies we can use to make pessimism work in our favor.

First, if yours is a mind that tends toward pessimism—that is, it tends to tell you that things will work out poorly—then it is wise to avoid the trap of dispositional pessimism. (That's the person that believes things will go badly and does nothing about it.) Instead, cultivate the skills of the defensive pessimist. When the mind says, *This plan isn't going to work*, ask yourself specifically how and why the wheels might fall off, and what you can do if specific problems arise.

Second, cultivate positive thoughts to balance the negative. The goal is not to eliminate or replace negative thoughts, but simply to create a more complete and coherent view of the situation.

In the case of the real estate agent who fears her sale may go sour, she can respond to her pessimistic thoughts by devising contingencies, as we've already discussed. But she can also try to identify the strong points and advantages within the situation. Perhaps the buyer wants something that the seller can easily provide, or maybe by examining the motives of each party she can identify a common goal.

The point is, we don't have to settle for the information that a biased mind provides automatically. We can also seek out our own information.

That brings us to a third strategy: accepting and responding thoughtfully to whatever the mind provides. Hosogoshi and Kodama (2009) found that defensive pessimists experience better health when they learn how to accept, rather than fight, their negative thoughts. They also noticed that people who become mired in fearful, depressive thoughts perceive little control over a situation. That prevents planning and saps motivation.

Acceptance doesn't extend just to thoughts. Skilled pessimists are also able to accept unpleasant feelings associated with their mind's gloomy prognostications. Defensive pessimists tend to perform best when they indulge their negative thoughts before they perform. Mark Seery and his colleagues (2008) point out that those negative predictions often come bundled with unpleasant feelings, but that those negative feelings actually facilitate preparatory performance.

But optimism is sometimes emotionally difficult, as well. While pessimism hurts before a performance, optimism can hurt afterward if the results aren't what the optimist anticipated. While defensive pessimists are rarely caught with their pants down, optimists are sometimes emotionally unprepared for defeat.

Pessimism, if we define it as the ability to spot potential problems and forecast trouble, is clearly hardwired into us. Some of us experience it more than others, but the thought that things will work out poorly can be some of our most emotionally charged and persuasive thoughts.

As always, when the mind tries to draw us into a chess match, we have more options than are readily apparent. The natural tendency is to play chess, either by submitting to the thoughts or by fighting against them. But there is always a third option: become the chessboard and simply notice what the mind is doing. It is calculating probabilities and helping us make the best possible mistakes in a world where mistakes are inevitable.

Whoever said "think positively" was overlooking the bright side of pessimism.

Pascal's Wager

Blaise Pascal was a French philosopher who believed that God's existence could not be proven with logic, but that a person should bet as if God exists. Working within the Judeo-Christian tradition, Pascal reasoned that living as if God exists places a person in the position to gain everything (heaven) if he is right and lose nothing (existence simply ceases) if he is wrong.

On the other hand, if one wagers that God does not exist, then he stands to lose everything if he is wrong (hell) and gain nothing if he is right. It's a sucker's bet. The best that can happen is breaking even.

Pascal believed that wagering is not optional. You must choose. Either you believe in God, or you do not. Betting that God does exist is, at a minimum, good risk management.

Despite its seeming detachment, there is beauty in Pascal's logic. It removes emotional judgment from the equation and highlights what is truly at stake. A person may not want to believe in God because he is angry, disillusioned, or simply rebellious. Pascal's analysis extracts the options and outcomes without the distraction of emotional evaluation.

Psychologist Kelly Wilson, who is influential in this book's discussion of values, puts a similar challenge to his fellow clinical psychologists (Wilson and DuFrene 2008). Either we can bet on the success of our clients and act as if they are going to succeed in all that they wish for, or we can bet that our clients will fail.

If we bet that our clients will succeed, committing our best service to them, then we stand to be part of something extraordinary. If we are wrong, then we feel bad and our clients feel bad, and that is the price we pay.

Suppose, on the other hand, that we bet against our clients. (And yes, some clinicians do that, perhaps to avoid disappointment.) Whether we turn out to be right or wrong, we have sold our clients short. And if our clients do not achieve something extraordinary (meaning we wagered correctly), then we get to enjoy the entirely hollow victory of being right.

Pascal's wager and Wilson's wager carry somewhat different contingencies. Incorrectly betting that God exists carries no real penalty in the Judeo-Christian tradition. If you are wrong, then existence ends and there is nothing—no punishment, no reward.

Incorrectly betting on the success of a client, however, *does* carry a penalty. It hurts to see someone struggle after becoming invested in their success. I like to believe that most clinicians will follow their values and bet on their clients' success anyway, with complete willingness to tolerate the pain of disappointment should they be incorrect.

Using an approach similar to Pascal's, this next exercise will help you gain distance from the mind's automatic pessimism so that you can use pessimistic thoughts to their best advantage and make informed choices.

Exercise: The Pessimism Contingency Table

Life is full of situations in which we are forced to choose a direction. As useful as pessimism can be, it is one more mental mechanism that can lead us away from our values if it runs unchecked. When the mind's default prediction is that things will go poorly, we need to apply extra effort in order to make sure we are moving in the direction of our values.

In those moments, we can follow Pascal's example and create a **contingency table,** which is a tool for illustrating the relationship between two or more variables.

For this exercise, recall a situation—preferably an ongoing one—in which you are experiencing pessimistic thoughts that collide with your values. Next, create a contingency table similar to the one in the illustration below.

By way of example, suppose you are considering reentering the dating scene after a painful breakup. Any well-functioning mind is going to scream, **Don't do it! The cost is too high! It is impossible to find true love!** But is it, really? When the mind speaks, it's generally a good policy to check the facts. In the case of pessimism, we want to know the true costs and benefits of our options. To accept the mind's evidence is to run the risk of moving away from what's important to us.

Date Again?

	Yes	No
Find an Ideal mate	Happiness with the risk of heartbreak.	Your perfect mate is looking for you, but he or she won't find you.
Find no mate	You experience heartbreak.	Continued loneliness. No heartbreak, no love.

It's important to be honest about the costs and benefits. Pessimistic thoughts are often quite vague. In our dating example, a person might experience thoughts such as **The cost of risking it again is too high.** Both "risking it" and "too high" are so vague as to be meaningless, but they sound quite ominous. Don't let your mind get away with vague, ominous threats. In this example, there is a very real possibility of experiencing heartbreak again. Is that price too high, as your mind insists? Only you can answer that question—but it's difficult to make a realistic appraisal when we are overwhelmed by ambiguous, dire thoughts.

This simple exercise can help us detach from the mind's evaluation of the outcomes. And once we know what's really at stake, our values can guide us. Some people may find it utterly unacceptable to risk heartache again, while other people's values compel them to embrace the risk of continued dating. The only right answer is the answer borne by your values.

Appreciating Pessimism

You can probably guess that my closing argument on pessimism is this: don't argue.

The world really is a dangerous place. Minds seem to know this. Some minds, more than others, want to address the problems in advance, and that's where pessimism comes in. Your particular degree of pessimism may have something to do with your history, and it may have something to do with disposition. But ultimately, perhaps it does not matter. Your mind does what it does.

Pessimistic thinking is so persuasive for some of us because it shows up as emotional impulses like hopelessness or fear. Pessimism also gains power from the fact that we tend to judge it harshly and fight against it. That only draws us further into the unwinnable chess game. You can gird yourself with the knowledge that you are not a slave to your pessimistic thoughts. You simply experience the mind's innate ability to calculate outcomes and the relative cost of errors. You might even thank your mind for that. It's pretty impressive, when you think about it.

Chapter 10

Quick Fixes

The mind has several powerful maneuvers at its command to keep us safe and moving in the right direction. Its selective use of history keeps us from falling into old snares, trump cards and double standards keep us in the good graces of others, and pessimistic thinking helps us manage risk in a dangerous world.

They all share something in common. They each have an intangible quality of compulsion, boosted at times by powerful emotions that are difficult to quantify and even more difficult to resist. Perhaps the mind's most powerful inducement is its desire to fix problems of comfort and safety, and to fix them *now*. The mind can drive us to "fix" our problems though complex behaviors like drinking, compulsive shopping, or seeking out shallow sexual relationships, but it can operate in subtler ways as well.

Consider Nancy, a woman at a dinner party who is uncomfortable with the formality of the gathering as well as the expectation that she mingle with strangers. That's a skill she has never developed. She stands awkwardly by herself, her social anxiety mounting, when a waiter glides by with a tray of crab puff hors d'oeuvres.

Nancy is on a strict diet and realizes that she will be sorely disappointed with herself if she eats one. She also knows from her own history that eating a single crab puff may start an unmanageable chain of overeating for the rest of the evening. Nevertheless, she finds herself reaching for the crab puffs and eating several of them, almost as if it were beyond her control. True to her own prediction, she overeats for the rest of the evening. The temptation was just too much.

She will later scold herself for breaking her diet, and she will truly feel bad for it. The same mind that compelled her to reach for that first crab puff will punish her with a hefty dose of shame for eating it. She will go to bed with a feeling of defeat, wondering why she has such an embarrassing lack of self-control.

But perhaps "lack of self-control" is not the most useful way to think about her behavior. Perhaps it would be more useful to look at this as problem-solving behavior. The mind is almost always looking out for us, even if it's shortsighted about doing so.

In Nancy's case, eating that first crab puff solved two problems. First, it solved the never-ending problem of obtaining calories. (It was a never-ending problem for our ancestors, at least, who would have gorged themselves on salty, fatty crab puffs because it might be weeks before they found more salt and fat.) Satisfying that urge simply feels good. And the mind likes things that feel good.

Second, and more subtly, eating the crab puff distracted her momentarily from the discomfort of her social anxiety. The avoidance of discomfort is one of the mind's primary objectives.

Eating that crab puff had two functions. It immediately removed pain while simultaneously adding pleasure—two rewards from a single behavior. It's no wonder Nancy's crab-puff compulsion was overpowering.

That duality of function propels problems ranging from overeating to addiction. It is an indelible characteristic of our minds, and overcoming it is one of the most difficult challenges the mind can present. And yes, this type of behavior begins with survival logic. When we're thirsty, it's our mind's job to make obtaining water the highest priority. When we're in pain, even emotional pain, our mind's job is to seek immediate relief.

In this chapter, we will look at how this survival logic functions and how you might respond to it. Often, and especially with matters such as addiction, it is most useful to seek professional help. But we will uncover some of the reasons the mind is so powerfully persuasive, and how it paradoxically adds so much fuel to the fire. Nancy's mind compelled her to do something that felt good and relieved anxiety, but in the end made her feel much worse.

How the Mind Competes with Itself

Sometimes it seems that the mind is a big bundle of competing impulses—and that may not be far from the truth. We do in fact find ourselves caught in an internal battle over contingencies. Our higher, rational minds pursue long-term goals while our primitive minds want immediate gratification.

What would happen if we removed one half of the equation and impeded one side or the other? If we muzzled our rational minds, would our primitive minds have free rein, or at least have more influence over us? The answer appears to be yes. That appears to be precisely one of the aftereffects of *traumatic brain injury* (TBI).

You might think of the *prefrontal cortex*—the area of the brain just above the eyes—as the seat of our higher, rational minds. It has been associated with judgment, reasoning, impulse control, and behavioral flexibility—or, in psychological shorthand, *executive functioning*. Due to its relatively isolated position in the brain and the proximity to bony structures inside the skull, the prefrontal cortex is particularly susceptible to injury from blows to the head or rapid acceleration such as might occur in a car accident.

When the frontal cortex is damaged, our ability to temper our responses suffers (Wood 2001). When our higher minds are cut off from our primitive minds and unable to regulate them, our behavior tends to become more impulsive.

Unlike the prefrontal cortex, the *limbic system* is buried deep within the brain and is better protected. This system contributes to impulse, drive, and emotional reaction—domains of the primitive mind. In a slightly

145

oversimplified explanation (there is much we don't know about TBI), we can think of some forms of TBI as an event that reduces our ability to curb our own impulses but leaves impulses intact. In other words, the emotional engine works, but the brakes are unreliable. Psychologists have labeled one grouping of behaviors stemming from injury to the prefrontal cortex the *executive dyscontrol syndrome*. Symptoms include irritability, impulsiveness, and reduced frustration tolerance (Smith 2006).

Phineas Gage, a man whose TBI is discussed in probably every introductory psychology course, offers a prototypical account of the social and behavioral difficulties that can follow TBI. Gage was working as the foreman of a railway construction gang in Cavendish, Vermont, when, on September 13, 1848, an accidental explosion sent a tamping iron through his head.

Gage's injury became the first reported case of severe damage to the ventromedial prefrontal cortex—much of the left frontal part of his brain was destroyed in the accident (Wagar and Thagard 2004). After his initial recovery, friends and family were dismayed to find that Gage was transformed from the gregarious, well-balanced, efficient foreman he once had been. He became profane, irreverent, unfocused, and unable to continue the job at which he had once excelled.

Mr. Gage's injury illustrates the modularity of the human brain and the fact that different systems sometimes act in opposition (the primitive mind urges us to lash out at someone with whom we're angry while the rational mind demands a more civil response). Left relatively unchecked, the primitive parts of Phineas Gage's mind ruled his behavior. His injury brought to the surface the thoughts, emotions, and impulses of the primitive mind.

We know that the primitive mind is a vast learning machine and that one of the ways in which it learns is by interacting with the environment and remembering how our actions influence the environment. This is the *antecedent-behavior-consequence* (ABC) model taught, along with the tale of Phineas Gage, in any respectable introductory psychology course.

For example, when a toddler notices a colorful row of candy at the grocery store checkout (antecedent), he might scream, "I want it, I want it, I want it!" (behavior) until his parents buy some candy for him (consequence). You can be sure that he'll remember that response and use the same behavior the next time the opportunity arises.

It seems that the mind tracks consequences at different levels, with the primitive mind compelling us toward immediate gratification, while the higher, rational mind compels us toward higher goals and long-term benefits. Nancy, at her dinner party, experienced just that. Her primitive mind saw crab puffs and shouted, metaphorically, "I want it, I want it, I want it!" while her rational, higher mind pushed for longer-term, more meaningful goals such as maintaining a healthy weight.

"I want it, I want it, I want it!" never goes away. The primitive mind is in constant pursuit of immediate gratification, and frequently it wins, as it did with Nancy.

But now let's get back to our original question—what would happen if we muzzled our rational minds and let the primitive mind run free? Wherever it has occurred, the primitive mind has shown its nature in full relief, as it did in the case of Phineas Gage. It illustrates by contrast the nature of our rational, higher minds. Our more evolved brain structures insulate us from the consequences of our own impulsiveness.

Conversely, we are equally hobbled, if not more so, without the drives of the primitive mind. Consider what happens when the amygdalae are damaged (those are the almond-shaped structures deep within our brains that we discussed in chapter 5). Animals that have suffered damage to these structures lose their fear of dangerous situations and become excessively docile, among other emotional and behavioral problems (Klüver and Bucy 1939). Humans who have suffered damage to the amygdalae also lose the ability to avoid risky monetary gambles, becoming willing to throw money away on sure losers (De Martino, Camerer, and Adolphs 2010). It's almost as if they had lost their useful pessimism.

The larger lesson here? Aside from the fact that gifts like fear and pessimism can be lost as easily as higher functions like tact and restraint, the primitive mind will always push us in primitive directions, and always toward immediate gratification. It will always urge us to take one more proverbial crab puff, long-term consequences be damned. It's up to us to keep one eye on the horizon, and to keep the primitive mind in check.

The Natural Drive for Immediate Gratification

Sometimes our internal struggles can be boiled down to a struggle between short-term and long-term consequences. Do we indulge in the small treat that will give us pleasure and diminish discomfort, or do we strive for higher, less tangible consequences?

We often choose short-term gain simply because long-term consequences are absent during moments of decision. When we are caught in discomfort or craving, short-term consequences dominate our immediate experience and have more control over our behavior (Ramnerö and Törneke 2008).

The drive for immediate gratification is evident among young children before they learn the invaluable and uniquely human skill of striving for more distant goals. In the late 1960s, psychologist Walter Mischel conducted one of the most famous experiments in psychology: he gave marshmallows to four- and five-year-olds. Of course, there were strings attached.

During the experiment, Dr. Mischel would bring the child into a room with a table and a marshmallow. He told the child that he would leave the room for fifteen minutes, during which time the child could eat the marshmallow. However, the child could have *two* marshmallows if he or she waited until he returned.

Only about 30 percent of the children were able to defer gratification and ignore the marshmallow on the table for fifteen minutes, which is a very long time for a young child. A few kids ate the marshmallow right away. The rest waited about thirty seconds, staring intently at the marshmallow before they ate it (Lehrer 2009).

The drive for immediate gratification can be so powerful that it overwhelms our better judgment. Intellectually, any child knows that two marshmallows are better than one, but in the heat of the moment the unyielding impulse of the primitive can be overwhelming. With age and experience, we learn to moderate its demands, but the primitive mind never goes away. It is always willing to take the bait whether or not we are better off forgoing the quick fix. Research like that of Walter Mischel gives us some insight into the most useful responses to such impulses.

Breaking the Quick-Fix Habit

In the battle over contingencies, it pays to keep the primitive mind in its place. Dr. Mischel's work was more than an interesting experiment on preschoolers' ability to delay gratification. He followed the children into young adulthood and noticed that the children who were able to hold out for two marshmallows tended to fare better in life. They did better in school, they were more able to pursue goals, and they had better self-control. They were more able to resist temptation, tolerate frustration, and cope with stress (Mischel, Shoda, and Rodriguez 1989). Though the primitive mind means well, clearly it does not always *do* well.

The recipe for breaking the habit of quick fixes is fairly straightforward, but not particularly easy. Denying a fixated mind is tricky business. Doing so requires resisting impulses without falling into the trap of thought suppression. We saw in chapter 1, for example, how suppressing thoughts about food can actually increase binge eating.

The more useful approach is to notice the impulse and choose a different behavior. Ignore it, but don't try to eliminate it. Treat it as if it were a noisy and annoying dog in the corner of the room. We don't have to respond; we can go about our business while it's in the room. Psychologists call this *exposure with response prevention* (ERP). We can bring ourselves in contact with a stimulus that has previously ruled our responses and deny ourselves immediate gratification.

It seems that is precisely what the successful 30 percent of children in Dr. Mischel's experiment did. One of the techniques the children relied on was what Dr. Mischel succinctly refers to as "strategic allocation of attention." Instead of fixating on the marshmallow, the children would distract themselves by covering their eyes, singing, or playing hide-and-seek under the table. We can be sure that they did not eliminate the desire for the marshmallow; they simply redirected their attention and did other things (Lehrer 2009).

By redirecting their own focus, the children accomplished something important. They insulated themselves from the sensual temptations of the marshmallow—the smell, the consistency, the powdery coating. They avoided the alluring features of the marshmallow. As far as we know, they did not attempt to avoid their thoughts, which are inescapable. They avoided the most enticing aspects of the marshmallow itself. (Marshmallows are avoidable. The desire for marshmallows is not.)

Avoiding those tempting features made it easier for the children to stay strong and pursue larger goals. The successful kids also shifted their focus from the sensual aspects of the tempting treat to the abstract, informational qualities. "If I wait, I get two." Shifting focus from the sensual to the intellectual components makes it easier to resist temptation (Mischel, Shoda, and Rodriguez 1989).

Redirecting their own attention and changing their focus when they thought of the marshmallow amounts to what Dr. Mischel calls "obscuring the temptation." Creating distance between oneself and the temptation reduces the odds of giving in (Quinn et al. 2010). The mind says, *Eat that crab puff! I want it, I want it, I want it!* to which we answer, *I won't get drawn into an argument, I'm walking away from the crab puff.*

Our desire for the crab puff or the marshmallow is almost incidental. Dr. Mischel's preschoolers taught us what matters most: how we respond to our own demanding, impulsive, quick-fixing minds. We may not be able to silence them, but we can ignore them, at least for a while. It gets easier with practice. Like muscles growing with exercise, with practice we can strengthen the systems that help us resist impulses. That skill seems to involve a bit of intentional avoidance.

Up to now, I have no doubt given the impression that avoidance is a dangerous thing. Really, it depends on what we are avoiding. We know from chapter 1 that avoiding our own thoughts and feelings is a dangerous path. The addict who uses drugs or alcohol to numb internal experiences will only require increasing amounts over time as shame, regret, depression, and anxiety mount. It's a losing battle.

But in this case, we're not talking about avoiding thoughts or feelings. As far as we know, the children in Mischel's marshmallow experiment made no effort to eliminate their desire for marshmallows, their thoughts about the marshmallows, or their anxiety about waiting for the marshmallows. As far as we know, they avoided nothing within their own minds.

The target of their avoidance existed outside their bodies and minds. They avoided certain aspects of the marshmallows. In some cases, they hid from the marshmallows. They did redirect their thoughts away from the sensual features of the marshmallows to the more abstract features of the situation, but redirection is not the same as dangerous thought-suppression. We can choose to focus our higher, rational minds on whatever we wish.

The children's avoidance was conscious and purposeful. Avoidance isn't always a bad thing, as long as we choose the target wisely. Let's look at three strategies for conscious and purposeful avoidance: obscure the temptation; stop the bus, I want to get off; and one shoe at a time.

1. Obscure the Temptation

When facing temptation, do what the children did. First, remove yourself, and do it quickly. When Nancy agonized, even briefly, about the crab puffs on the waiter's tray, she gave herself time to notice how tempting they were. She caught a whiff of the little delicacies, noticed their texture, and began to imagine what they would taste like. She unintentionally made herself acutely aware of just how satisfying it would be to eat them. She allowed her mind a glimpse of the immediate gratification at her fingertips—and we know how powerful immediate consequences are.

Next, focus your attention on the abstract qualities of the situation. Nancy might have taken a moment to give herself a pep talk about her diet and her goals.

One of the very first things you might do when confronted with temptation is take a break. Run away. Go to the restroom, run outside, do something to change your physical situation. Then you'll be able to see the situation with some rationality, and your mind won't be running the show all by itself.

2. Stop the Bus, I Want to Get Off

Sometimes we don't make it over that first hump. We fail to obscure the temptation and find ourselves in the midst of indulging our mind's impulses. Sometimes we're already eating the crab puffs before we even realize it.

Those are discouraging moments, and they will occur. *I've already eaten three crab puffs and ruined my diet,* says the mind. *I may as well give up.* But we need not continue down the road simply because we've already started.

When that happens, stop. Take a time-out. Remove yourself from the situation. Assess your values and the long-term consequences. It is never too late to change course. Change comes in fits and starts, and very few of us master temptations on the first try.

If your mind is saying something like *You've already failed, so you might as well continue,* closely examine the usefulness of that thought. Even if the damage is done, you can at the very least practice stopping. Every time you do it, you get better at it. Any time is a good time for success.

3. One Shoe at a Time

Sometimes immediate gratification exists in *not* doing something—staying home from the gym, avoiding homework, or escaping a difficult conversation. When the mind stubbornly refuses to move forward, drawing your attention instead to the sensual and pleasing aspects of avoidance (*Wouldn't it feel great to eat cookies rather than go to the gym?*), it often helps to break the task down into small steps.

Anyone who is avoiding something like going to the gym can easily become overwhelmed at the thought of the task. Instead, focus on the smaller steps involved. Put one shoe on. Then the next. Then walk to the car, and so on. If you draw your attention away from the big picture and focus instead on small, achievable tasks, soon enough you will have completed your workout in spite of your mind's best efforts to spare you from the pain of it.

Managing the Drive for Quick Fixes

Sometimes the mind seeks immediate gratification to quell an appetite. *I want a salty, fatty treat, and I want it now.* Other times, the mind seeks immediate gratification of a different form: reduction of tension or anxiety. Though there are different physical systems involved than those we have discussed previously, the mind still seeks a quick fix.

Obsessive-compulsive disorder (OCD) exemplifies the quick fix of tension reduction in the extreme. The symptoms include "recurrent obsessions or compulsions that are severe enough to be time-consuming or cause marked distress or significant impairment" (American Psychological Association 2000). The APA estimates that between 0.5 and 2.1 percent of people across cultures experience the symptoms at some point in their lives. If you have OCD yourself, you need no explanation of the anguish this problem brings.

OCD is like a battle between a rational, higher mind and a primitive mind. The primitive mind has learned that certain ritualized behaviors, like washing hands or checking locks, can provide brief relief from anxiety. The higher mind knows the cost for doing so increases with each succession. Work goes undone, relationships suffer, and the seeming irrationality of it feels embarrassing. (There is nothing irrational about it, from the mind's point of view. If the behavior reduces anxiety and discomfort, then it is successful.)

The struggle of OCD can feel like a battle raging within. The mind insists on performing the behavior it knows will reduce discomfort (albeit very temporarily), while the rational mind tallies up the costs of doing so. And like the dog at the back fence wearing a path as it frantically barks at each innocuous passing stranger, the mind's OCD habit gets stronger with each repetition.

Like any other mind, the mind with OCD wants to know that it is safe. But in this case, it has come to associate safety with ritualized thoughts and behaviors, which it demands repeatedly. The easiest way to quiet the mind is to give in to its demands. That eases the pressure briefly, but just like the dog at the back fence, the mind doesn't stay satisfied for long.

The mind with OCD is really no different from any other mind—it just provides more anxiety and demands more action than other minds. Though its fundamental nature cannot be changed (all minds worry), the obsessive-compulsive mind can be trained.

As one more demonstration of the modularity of the mind—and how we can use that to our advantage—let's take a brief look at some of the wiring behind OCD.

OCD involves several specific brain structures, including the *caudate nuclei,* which lie deep within each hemisphere. In brain images of patients with OCD, these areas burn abnormally high amounts of energy (Linden 2006). Brain imaging also suggests that this little corner of the primitive mind can be trained. Successful talk therapy reduces OCD symptoms as the caudate nuclei return to a more normal level of baseline activity. Why?

Treatment for OCD involves denying the mind's impulses for immediate gratification and redirecting activity. (Sound familiar? Dr. Mischel's kids would approve.) It is a bit like refusing to allow a dog to engage in panic at the back fence. The dog (and the mind) will at first protest and experience increased anxiety, but can you blame them? They're only trying to avoid catastrophe, or so they assume.

If we take charge, offer reassurance, and redirect the dog, it will eventually learn that things usually turn out okay without all the ruckus. Similarly, the primitive mind can be taught that things will turn out okay without engaging in ritualized thoughts and behaviors that give the illusion of effectiveness. Washing one's hands until they bleed does not solve problems, but to the primitive mind it can certainly appear to work that way because of the immediate relief from anxiety. Seeing past that illusion requires difficult exposure to the facts. Just as people can exert top-down control over dogs, we can use our higher minds to overrule the demands of our primitive minds.

There Is No Off Switch, But There Is Hope

Sometimes the mind wants to be in charge and to lead us away from our values. It wants the pendulum of our experience to swing in a small, safe arc. Safety first.

The more primitive parts of the mind don't always understand what our higher minds are trying to accomplish. They hold disconnected, sometimes opposing motives. When the mind notices that we need its help—when the pendulum is swinging too wide—it steps in whether or not we want it to. And it has powerful tools at its disposal.

The mind's memory of pain and danger is nearly infallible. It can immobilize us even when we understand intellectually that it is safe to proceed. But it can accomplish that only when we forget to keep an eye on it, compassionately accept all that it gives us, and keep ourselves firmly grounded in our higher values. Ultimately, living with a primitive mind means strengthening the ability to ignore its demands and move on.

I hope this chapter has offered you some useful strategies for responding to quick-fix impulses. Occasionally, these impulses turn into habits and addictions that defy our best efforts to manage them. If you are struggling with an addicted or painfully anxious mind, it makes sense to seek professional help.

So far, we have discussed how the mind works, how to observe it, and how to disobey it in the pursuit of higher values. While the mind sometimes tries to overpower us, it can also sneak up on us when our defenses are down. Now, in the final section of this book, let's turn our attention toward keeping our higher minds in good repair in order to prevent ambush.

Part 4

Mood, Lifestyle, and Psychological Flexibility

The mythical Greek figure Tantalus had a promising career as a ruler of men until he chose to offend the gods. For starters, he stole their ambrosia for his people. Then he sealed his fate by offering his son, Pelops, as a sacrifice. He cut the child into pieces and served him to the gods in a Pelops stew. These were unwise moves by someone who had once been welcome at the table of Zeus. The gods were displeased, to say the least. His punishment was forever to crave delights that were just beyond his reach.

The gods cast Tantalus into a clear, cool lake from which he could never drink. When he tried to take the water, it would recede from him, leaving only thick, black mud at his feet. Above his head were low branches containing wonderful fruit. As soon as he reached for the fruit, a gust of wind would blow it just beyond his reach. And so Tantalus exists to this day in the deepest realm of the underworld, forever tantalized and tortured.

Our own minds can place us in a situation similar to that of Tantalus when they forbid from us from seeking that which we most desire. Relationships, activities, or whatever else our values demand can seem unattainable for hours, weeks, or most of a lifetime. The culprit is not a god on Olympus. It is often our own mood.

Mood can alter our perception of the environment and of ourselves. It can diminish our sense of control over our world. It can even alter our memory. A low mood can put our mind in the driver's seat, keeping us perfectly safe and perfectly miserable. But unlike poor Tantalus, we need not resign ourselves to eternal deprivation. By understanding how our moods function, and by embracing a lifestyle that lessens our vulnerability to the vagaries of mind and mood, we gain psychological flexibility and the freedom to pursue our cherished values.

Chapter 11

Welcome to Your
State of Mind

I t's perfectly normal to feel like an entirely different person, with entirely different options, when mood grabs hold of the mind and colors perception. Moods can become pervasive and constant, or they can fluctuate with troubling frequency. In Mallory's case, mood quite literally influenced the course of her life.

Mallory's Mood

At just thirty-four years of age, Mallory has done well for herself professionally. She manages an efficient and responsive information technology department in a large accounting firm. She is respected and sought after, and she makes an admirable salary. Her job also brings her a different kind of comfort, of which she is only vaguely aware: her position defines the boundaries and parameters of her relationships. It insulates her from others. Or, at least, she allows it to.

Mallory is a profoundly private person. The only place she is forced to interact with others is at work, and so it's no coincidence that she finds herself at a demanding and socially formal company. Professionalism and the prim culture allow her to maintain congenial but arm's-length relationships with her subordinates and coworkers. Mallory is thankful for those boundaries. She fears that without them, the old patterns might reemerge.

In her previous jobs, Mallory came to be known as moody, distant, and asocial. Sometimes people referred to her as "the office bitch." She laughed off the pain, boasting that she was the most organized bitch in the county, but she joked only to avoid the pain those comments brought. Joking was simpler than fighting for what she truly wanted.

Contrary to appearances, she desperately wanted to connect with her coworkers. She wanted to laugh with them after hours, to be invited to social gatherings, and to participate in their playful water-cooler banter. But it all seemed so distant and unattainable. Something nameless stood in her way. It came from within, and it exhausted her. Day after day, she fought the thoughts and feelings, and she was left so weary there was room for little else in her life.

Mallory once confided in a relative that she has been in a bad mood since high school. For most of her adult life, she has suffered what psychologists refer to as *dysthymia*—a chronic low mood that fails to meet the criteria for major depression. Along with it, she experiences thoughts that she despises but cannot easily prevent.

Mallory expects the worst from people and from herself, even though she wishes she were more optimistic. She notices mainly anger and hostility in others, even though she knows she should look for the good in people. She even has difficulty recalling anything but the worst experiences in her own past, even though she feels she should be more appreciative of her life. She feels like a ghost walking though the world of the living, never quite able to see things as others do or to experience the richness of life. Everything and everyone is muted and distorted by her mood.

And so, believing that the richness of life simply lies beyond her grasp, Mallory has arrived at a good-enough solution. By finding a professional position that insulates her from familiarity and intimacy, she hides in plain sight. She has found isolation in the crowd and functions admirably, by all appearances. Here she is seen merely as distant. Here she almost fits in.

Don't Trust Every Mood You Meet

Mood and perception are inexorably intertwined, it seems. Perception affects our mood and, as we'll examine in some detail, mood affects perception.

Perception and Context: How the Mind Filters Information

Perception is a tricky thing. The information that percolates up through the modules of the mind and into our consciousness may not be as reliable as it seems. One of the effects of mood is to alter our perception in some ways that reinforce and sustain the same mood that is altering our perception to begin with.

Context has a strong effect on the information that our minds make most readily available. For instance, a person might have difficulty recalling someone's identity when they encounter them outside their usual context—it's confusing to encounter someone at the grocery store when previously we've seen them only at the building in which we work.

To test the effects of context, Viorica Marian and Margarita Kaushanskaya (2007) conducted an experiment in which they questioned bilingual English and Mandarin speakers in both languages. In one question, they asked participants to name a statue of someone standing with a raised arm while looking in the distance. When that question was asked in Mandarin, the participants were more likely to describe a famous statue of Mao Zedong; when the question was asked in English, they were more likely to describe the Statue of Liberty. The researchers also noticed that the participants more easily recalled information when they were tested in the same language in which they had originally learned the information.

What's the importance of this type of finding? It suggests that the mind filters and selects information for us based on relevancy and association.

Information that reaches our rational, higher minds has been processed by areas of the brain that mediate attention and memory. Unfortunately, the information provided by the mind is not always the most accurate or useful. When we encounter that work-related acquaintance at the grocery store, it would be nice if the mind provided us with their name or our relationship to them. Such is not always the case.

One bit of context that seems to have a profound impact on perception is mood. One of the most compelling definitions of mood comes from Sadock and Sadock's (2003) *Synopsis of Psychiatry*. They define it as "a pervasive and sustained emotion that colors the person's perception of the world."

Context is not confined to external variables, such as location or time. Context includes our own internal states, and mood is a powerful prism through which to view the world. Information colored by emotion can be remarkably unreliable. Mood can alter our perception like a new lens on a camera can alter the pictures it takes. Sometimes a mind under the influence of mood is simply not to be trusted.

How Mood Colors Perception

Moods can color and distort our perception of the world in specific ways that often perpetuate the mood we're already in. This may be part of the reason Mallory became so stuck. The longer she sees the world through her prism of mood, the stronger the prism becomes. And the prism of low mood can literally be quite narrowing. It can even affect our visual perception.

Yana Avramova and colleagues (2010) noticed that happy people typically have a broader visual scope, focusing more on global features of the visual field. They also display a more open mind-set. Sad people, on the other hand, rely on a narrower visual scope, focusing on specific features of the visual field. Sad people also display a more detail-oriented, analytic mind-set.

While we may intuitively judge the "happy" visual style to be better, Avramova and colleagues make no such supposition. Each visual style is useful. They hypothesize that negative moods, which probably exist to alert us to dangers in the environment, are naturally accompanied by a visual style that is more selective and vigilant. Positive mood, which broadens the perceptual field, is the mind's signal that the environment is benign. We can relax a little and take it all in.

What does this mean on a daily basis? Since our minds literally expand and contract visual perception, we may be prone to certain types of mistakes. We may miss relevant details when we're flying high; we may miss important contextual cues when we're in the gutter.

The latter error can perpetuate low mood. We may notice a frown on someone's face while overlooking the reason behind it. We may leave with the impression that the person was grumpy for no good reason, and too much of that makes the world an ugly place.

This perceptual bias, by itself, is not terribly dramatic, and it doesn't apply equally to everyone. It's not as if we develop sudden and profound tunnel vision when our mood drops, but visual focus is one of the many subtle mood-based influences on our perception. There are others.

Schmid and Mast (2010) noticed that people in negative moods more easily recognize negative facial expressions from others. They also had more difficulty recognizing happy facial expressions than people in a neutral mood. People in positive moods, on the other hand, have more difficulty recognizing sad facial expressions. We seem to have slightly more difficulty recognizing the moods of others when they differ from our own feelings. This is yet another perceptual distortion that perpetuates mood.

Researchers have found another mood-perpetuating effect. We more easily learn information that is congruent with our current mood. When we're sad, we attend more to sad information. Because we attend to it, we more easily recall it (Blaney 1986). We also recall things more easily when we're in the same mood in which we learned the information (Kenealy 1997). When we're sad, we more easily recall the sad times, and when we're angry, we are more likely to recount hostile stories and find fault with others (Bower 1981).

This mood-based mediating of the information to which we attend makes mood self-perpetuating. Through no fault or intention, a mind like Mallory's can spend a lifetime gathering information that feeds sadness.

Mood also affects our receptivity to messages. Rene Ziegler (2010) noted that people in both good and bad moods scrutinized messages less thoroughly. They're more gullible than people in neutral moods. Ziegler also pointed out that we tend to be more skeptical when a message is incongruent with our mood. Conversely, we are more accepting of information consistent with our current mood.

And if that weren't enough, mood also affects memory. A depressed mood reduces recall of *episodic memory* (the recall of specific life events), so that our own history is more difficult to conjure (Ellis et al. 1985). Even our *implicit memory* (things we have learned without realizing we have learned them) is biased by negative mood. When we feel low, we tend to recall negatively tinged information (Watkins et al. 1996).

This can be yet another insidious way in which depression begets depression. If we attend a job interview while in a low mood, we may fail to notice the mind churning away in the background, recalling bad interview experiences and influencing our behavior.

To make matters worse, trying to suppress moods is no more productive than trying to suppress thoughts. (And we've seen how well that works— remember my difficulty in not thinking of monkeys?) Attempts at mood suppression can actually make moods worse, particularly when our minds are preoccupied with troubling thoughts. Ironically, our minds are likely to be preoccupied when we're in a bad mood (Dalgleish et al. 2009). Moods, and bad moods in particular, can become quite circular and self-sustaining. Just ask Mallory.

Managing Bad Moods

So what's a person to do with these perception-clouding, memory-impairing, judgment-fouling, self-sustaining moods? We should not simply lie there and take it, but extricating ourselves from a string of bad moods takes patience, effort, and some counterintuitive action.

Perhaps it begins with our old, familiar recipe: noticing what the mind is doing, appreciating the beauty and the function of it, and deciding whether or not it's useful at the moment. Freeing oneself from low mood is rather like escaping quicksand. The more we struggle, the worse it gets. The secret is to lean into the pain and accept that perhaps the mind is not to be trusted when it is engaged in the business of coloring perception.

Far from being bad news, there is much hope in the possibility that our minds are lovingly misleading us. I think it's wonderful news! With that knowledge comes the hope that perhaps—just perhaps—my mind *might* be wrong this time. With that comes the hope and possibility of seeing beyond what the mind provides, as well as the hope that a better day will come.

My Mind Might Be Wrong

Accepting what the mind offers—moods and all—can pay real dividends. Amanda Shallcross and her colleagues (2010) noticed that emotional acceptance is much more than a feel-good philosophical platitude. It is an effective coping strategy, even when our bad moods are in direct response to life difficulties. Shallcross found that accepting unpleasant emotions decreases negative affect, even during difficult times. Many people have told me that they fear their emotions will spin out of control if they allow themselves to experience them. Quite the opposite seems to be true.

Accepting negative emotions must also mean accepting the possibility that perception may be tainted, and that what the mind says may not be trustworthy. That can be a difficult task. Humans typically abhor ambiguity. The mind compels us to understand, especially when it believes that there is a problem that must be solved. But it is possible to sit with ambiguity, and sometimes it can be quite useful.

That was certainly true for a client of mine who sought help for her depression. She would feel fine for a time, until some stressful event in her life put her in a low mood. Her periods of low mood were accompanied by fairly paranoid thoughts. When she was depressed, she assumed that others harbored ill will toward her, and she assumed the worst in their intentions. Once a coworker innocently invited her to lunch. My client, suffering through a depressive phase, assumed that the woman had invited her in order to gain information that she could later use for blackmail or manipulation.

But it was her difficulties with her boyfriend that ultimately brought her to my office. During her depressed periods, she found herself making unfounded accusations. She felt as if there was an entirely different person inside of her who took over during her darkest moments, twisting innocuous words and actions of others into nefarious plots.

During her depressive periods, she had difficulty seeing the inaccuracy of her thoughts. Augmented by low mood and distorted perception, they felt entirely real. With practice, using the kinds of observing techniques we discussed in earlier chapters of this book, she learned to grasp onto the possibility that her mind *just might* be wrong. While her thoughts felt real during her depressed phases, she knew that the very same thoughts had recently felt false, and that they would feel false again in the near future. That was enough to keep her from taking the thoughts too seriously.

Knowing the thoughts and mood would pass, and identifying which kinds of thoughts were untrustworthy—thoughts such as *My boyfriend will never understand me* or *He's intentionally hurting my feelings to drive me away*— made her moods much more tolerable. Even in her darkest moments, experience told her it would pass. Not surprisingly, her depressed moods decreased in frequency and intensity. It took practice, but eventually the old thoughts simply didn't bother her very much. Like an annoying commercial on the radio, she knew her thoughts would soon enough move along, and so there was no need to indulge them or respond to them.

Back in chapter 3, we discussed the racetrack metaphor. With practice, we can learn to observe our minds as if watching racecars from the stands. Moods can make it exceptionally difficult to observe the mind. Bad moods can demand that we become a driver in the race rather than an observer in the stands. Rather than dispassionately watching our thoughts go by, we are desperately trying to avoid a crash.

In those moments, we can begin to extricate ourselves from the race—we can begin to loosen our mind's grip on us—by grasping on to the possibility that our minds *just might* be wrong.

Life doesn't allow us to simply wait for our minds to line up with reality. We must act in the world. We must go to work, participate in relationships, and otherwise live our lives. The question we face in our darkest moments is whether or not to act on information from our depressed, misperceiving minds—information that might be wrong.

Opposite Action: Moving Toward Values

In chapter 6, we discussed values: how to define them and how to move toward values when the mind pushes in another direction. It all looks good on paper, but a depressed mood can greatly complicate the pursuit of values. Consider Mallory. Her values include close connection with others, but for years her mood has stood like a brick wall blocking her way. Mallory's values have become a distant memory. Reclaiming them will take dutiful effort, but it can be done.

One of the most useful techniques I have found for jump-starting values is *opposite action* from Marsha Linehan's (1993) dialectical behavior therapy. While her therapy is designed for people with serious relational difficulties, many of the techniques, including opposite action, are just plain good practices for anyone.

In concept, opposite action is simple: follow the opposite of our emotional impulses when those impulses have harmed us in the past. When mood and values are in conflict, ignore mood and follow values.

In practice, opposite action can be a difficult challenge because the mind does *not* like to be disobeyed. As we discussed in earlier chapters, our minds can meet our resistance with punishing anxiety. I have found it useful to start small with opposite action.

Let's look at Mallory's situation. Her values tell her to connect with her coworkers, but her mood pushes her in the opposite direction. Her mood also affects her perception and she experiences thoughts that reinforce and justify her self-imposed isolation. *Don't bother talking to them; they obviously don't want to talk to you.*

For Mallory, opposite action would mean defying her mood-based thoughts and urges in order to get closer to others. If she were to start small, she might simply approach, rather than avoid, a group of coworkers as they chat in the break room—a small act she will never commit if she continues to follow her mood. With practice, it will become increasingly easier to (1) identify the discrepancies between her mood and her values, and (2) follow her values instead of her emotions.

Yes, it will be difficult. She is out of practice, she will be anxious, and she may feel awkward as she tries to act in a values-consistent manner for the first time in many years. Luckily, we humans are tough, resourceful, and resilient. She has survived many years of misery; she can certainly handle the discomfort of acting in opposition to her mind, especially if she starts small. Where lost values are concerned, sometimes we need to learn how to walk before we can run.

To paraphrase Dr. Linehan (Rizvi and Linehan 2005), there are a couple of tips for successfully implementing opposite action. The first is to remember that the goal is simply to identify a troubling emotion and respond to it in a novel way, not to suppress it. The second is to embrace opposite action fully, right down to implementing the right facial expression and ignoring unconstructive thoughts.

In Mallory's case, that might mean ensuring that she smiles, speaks cheerfully, and makes good eye contact when she approaches her coworkers in the break room. These things may not come naturally. Full commitment would also mean noticing and ignoring (but not suppressing) whatever bleak or critical thoughts appear as she takes those first few steps toward value-driven action. Now let's see how opposite action might work in your life.

Exercise: Opposite Action

For this exercise, identify a situation in your life in which you are not acting in accordance with your values, perhaps because your mind puts up emotional roadblocks like Mallory's depressed mood.

Following Mallory's example, identify one or two small steps you can take to begin acting in the service of your values. It's important to start small. Recall that Mallory probably should not begin by hosting dinner parties or other large social events. Instead, her initial goal might be simply to approach a group of coworkers rather than avoid them as her mind and her mood insist that she do.

Once you have identified a small goal, make plans to make it happen. Pick a time and place, if possible, and decide what you want to accomplish. Mallory, for example, might ask herself to say hello, smile, and make eye contact with a few people rather than trying to engage them in an extended conversation the first time.

As you engage in opposite action, know that your mind will protest. You may experience anxiety, painful thoughts, and any number of emotions.

Remind yourself to see them for what they are: nothing more than activities of the mind. They will pass.

Finally, after you have completed the exercise, write about the experience. Remember it's important to put words to our internal experiences so that we do not become overwhelmed by the vague, ominous thoughts and feelings that minds are so good at creating. Was violating your mind's rules worth the effort? Did it bring you closer to your values? Would it be useful to do it again? Only you can answer those questions.

To Medicate or Not to Medicate?

What about antidepressants? Are they a good option for someone in Mallory's position? It depends. Low mood and depression come in many flavors, and proper diagnosis is crucial to effective treatment.

For problems like the condition known as major depression, antidepressant medication may be the best option. On the other hand, someone in Mallory's position may be better off with talk therapy alone. Addressing the problems that lie behind depression is often more effective and longer lasting than medication (Dobson et al. 2008).

Drugs aren't always the first or best answer. In fact, there is compelling evidence that antidepressants are routinely misused in Western countries. Researchers Jon Jureidini and Anne Tonkin (2006) found that many prescriptions (one third or more, depending on the measure and the population) fell outside clinical indications, were given in excessive doses, or were prescribed for unduly prolonged periods.

According to another study, only about one-third of patients experience relief after taking an antidepressant for a sufficient period (Cascade, Kalali, and Blier 2007). I suspect that has more to do with poor diagnosis than the effectiveness of antidepressants, because medications also seem to be under-prescribed among patients who might benefit the most. In addition to their data on overprescription, Jureidini and Tonkin noted that fewer than 25 percent of US, Canadian, and European patients meeting criteria for major depression receive appropriate medication management.

Antianxiety medication is equally tricky. Anxiety also comes in many varieties. If the underlying source of it isn't properly identified, then improper medication can actually serve to strengthen the anxiety by contributing to a pattern of avoidance. As we discussed in chapter 5, patterns of avoidance almost always make anxiety worse.

Psychiatric medications can literally save lives in the right circumstance, and they can be a futile waste of effort when used incorrectly. They can even make things worse. Proper diagnosis and treatment requires a thorough inter-view from an experienced mental health professional. That requires effort, which is difficult in the midst of anxiety and depression, but careful diagnosis is a sound investment that can lead to proper treatment.

Moods have a unique way of grabbing hold of our behavior and forcing us away from our values, but it need not be that way. We can chip away the influence of our moods by recognizing their illusory and transient nature. We can take steps toward our values through opposite action. In the right circum-stance, we can even benefit from medication. In the next and final chapter, we'll look at lifestyle choices that help to insulate us from the overpowering nature of thoughts and feelings.

Chapter 12

Mind the Basics

Luke, Penelope, Andy, and Mallory—the composite case studies in this book—share a universal struggle. Call it a hindrance from within. They each want to live their lives, while their minds, with all the best intentions, stand in the way. Like benevolent but overbearing big brothers, these minds are only trying to help. Our protagonists are caught in an internal tug-of-war. Safety and predictability lie at one end, and their values at the other.

That struggle creates equilibrium of a sort. As long as we stay engaged in the battle with our own minds, we reduce the chances of being badly hurt. But stagnation is the price we pay for too much safety. Luke wanted connection; his mind drove him to avoid the pain of rejection. Penelope wanted a vibrant life; her mind demanded she avoid the dangers of the world. Andy wanted closeness with his spouse; his mind sought the comfort and predictability of old patterns. Mallory wanted to be spirited and outgoing; her mind poisoned her perceptions in pursuit of shelter from ill-defined threats.

Their ultimate commonality is they are not controlling their own destinies and they are not making their own choices. They accept what little is left over from the inner conflict that has come to define their worlds.

The idea of inner conflict is nothing new. Sigmund Freud long ago wrote about conflict between the savage id and the moral superego. Perhaps the best-known example is Freud's notion of the Oedipus complex, in which a young man subconsciously fantasizes about killing his father so that he may possess his mother. Knowing that murder is wrong, the young man compromises by emulating his father's nature so he may more honorably earn his mother's approval. In Freud's scheme, failure to resolve that inner conflict could result in any number of serious neuroses.

Such early theories have rightly fallen out of favor, but the idea of a mind in conflict with itself seems to be quite literally true, from competing modules to competing neurons. The more we study the brain, the more we learn about its inner battles.

We have already seen examples of specific structures overstepping their bounds within the brain. (Think back to the hyperactive caudate nuclei and their role in obsessive-compulsive disorder that we discussed in chapter 10). Even at the level of individual neurons, the brain seems to be in a constant struggle with itself, and that may be by design.

Our brains possess some fancy mechanisms for gating neuronal signals (allowing some signals to proceed while stopping others) when one group of neurons says *stop!* and another says *go!* (Vogels and Abbot 2009; Kremkow, Aertsen, and Kumar 2010). Freud might have been interested to know that improper gating of neuronal signals has been identified in some forms of anxiety (Snyder et al. 2010).

Sigmund Freud may be considered misguided in some quarters, but he was remarkably perceptive when he theorized about inner conflict. The only thing he lacked was our most recent century's findings with which to refine his observations.

It seems that the brain intentionally tries to slow us down for purposes ranging from efficient functioning to staying safe in a dangerous world. And that brings us back to the topic of mood. Slowing us down and changing our focus seems to be one of the adaptive functions of low moods. That's all well and good until it impedes our values and our psychological flexibility.

Discover When You Are Most Vulnerable to the Mind

Returning to the last chapter's thesis for a moment, our perception of things cannot always be trusted. We perceive the world as a stable and predictable landscape, when in fact the information percolating up through the brain and into our consciousness frequently offers a skewed view of things.

Mallory was in a clear conflict with her mind. She wanted to follow her values while her mind had different plans. With her perception of others, herself, and even her own history altered by a depressed mood, her social life dwindled away. Since it's a given that the mind will present us with such conflicts sooner or later, it pays to know how minds work in general. Just as importantly, it pays to understand the quirks and limitations of our own individual minds.

Each of us has certain situations in which we are vulnerable to the mind's efforts to decrease our flexibility and pull us away from our values. This author's mind, for example, is not to be trusted at certain times of the day. It's almost as if I possess two distinctly different minds—one for the early morning, and another that comes out late at night.

My morning mind is irritable and uncreative and tends to see the worst in people. My nighttime mind is recklessly enthusiastic. It is hard to decide which of them possesses the worse judgment, and it's an odd experience when morning mind wonders what the hell the overenthusiastic nighttime mind was thinking the night before. With a lot of practice, I've learned to recognize and ignore them both.

There are certain precautions we can take against the mind's perceptual changes. Most are common sense, though sometimes difficult to recognize. If your mind is an anxious one, don't drink caffeine. If your mind is a depressed one, avoid alcohol. If your mood is particularly susceptible to low blood glucose levels, eat frequently.

There are also more abstract components of lifestyle, such as social contact. If your mood dips when you're isolated, then make sure you have plenty of social contact. You might search for a job in customer service rather than computer programming.

Those types of lifestyle choices may seem obvious from a distance, but they are terribly easy to overlook. That's why many 12-step recovery programs use the acronym HALT. It's a reminder that those in recovery should not allow themselves to become too Hungry, Angry, Lonely, or Tired. Conditions like those can sneak up on people, making them unwittingly susceptible to the mind's influence.

While each mind is different, there are three things in particular that can lower our immunity to the mind: poor diet, lack of exercise, and insufficient sleep. I've seen them crop up in my practice time and again, contributing greatly to mood and anxiety problems.

How Healthy Habits Insulate Us from the Mind

Proper diet, sleep, and exercise can minimize bad moods and distorted perceptions, and they can help us resist a mind that is dragging us away from our values. It's simple enough in concept, but these three lifestyle categories are easily trumped by the primitive mind's inclination toward short-term relief. When we're feeling down, the things that are best for us can be the last things we want to do. Who wants to exercise, eat a balanced meal, and go to bed early after a difficult day? It's so much more rewarding—at least in the short term—to curl up in front of the TV with pizza and a beer. Ah, sweet relief!

Yet habits like those give the primitive mind more power over us, and they weaken our ability to distance ourselves from its thoughts and feelings.

Diet

I am certainly no nutritionist. For many years, I operated under the half-joking theory that my body could synthesize any necessary nutrient from a bag of chips and a candy bar. And I wondered why I had no energy. Aside from the lack of a healthful, balanced diet, there are three substances that appear consistently in my practice to make life unnecessarily difficult for my clients: sugar, caffeine, and alcohol. Getting these substances under control usually makes life with a human mind much simpler.

SUGAR

In their 2002 study, Arthur Westover and Lauren Marangell pointed out a highly significant correlation between refined sugar consumption and annual rates of depression. While they were careful not to draw a causal relationship between sugar and depression, the more one consumes, the likelier it is that depression will strike. Our ancestors, according to the researchers, learned to crave sugar some thirty-five million years ago, but refined sugar was unknown in Central Europe until the sixteenth century.

Apparently, we're designed to crave sugar because it is difficult to obtain in the natural environment—but we are not built to freely consume it.

There is a hypothesis that people with a tendency toward low mood seek out sugar and simple carbs because these provide an increase in the neurotransmitter serotonin. An increase in serotonin, in turn, gives a temporary mood boost. People prone to feeling unhappy tend to crave carb-rich meals, and they tend to report improvements in their mood after eating (Corsica and Spring 2008).

But people who seek out simple carbs may be achieving the opposite in the long run. A blast of sugar causes the body to neutralize the sugar and can ultimately result in lower blood glucose. That can lead to low mood and irritability, especially when performing cognitively demanding tasks (Benton 2002). That, in turn, can lead to a craving for more sugar. You can see how a vicious cycle of roller-coaster mood swings might result, making a person particularly susceptible to unpleasant perceptions and thoughts.

The answer? Provide the body and mind with a steady flow of energy. Complex carbohydrates, like whole grains, are slow to digest and produce a steady flow of energy. A study by Felice Jacka and colleagues (2010) found that women who consume a diet of fruits, vegetables, meats, and whole grains have a lower incidence of depression than those who consume a diet high in fried and processed foods.

What's right for you? Talk to a nutritionist, and do some experimenting to find out what works best. In my experience, people who change their diets from highly processed, sugary foods to a good balance of complex carbohydrates, protein, and fats notice improvements in their mood and anxiety problems. At the very least, they're better equipped to view their thoughts from a safe distance.

CAFFEINE

The American Psychiatric Association (2000) reported that caffeine use is "ubiquitous" in the United States, with an average daily intake of 200 milligrams, and up to 30 percent of Americans consuming more than 500 milligrams or more.

What's not to love about caffeine? It boosts energy and improves some aspects of cognition. An early study into the effects of caffeine found that it increased work production by 7 percent in a stationary bike test, while the participants' perception of work output remain unchanged (Ivy et al. 1979).

Most of us can handle caffeine with little problem, but people who struggle with certain types of anxiety, like panic disorder or performance or social anxiety, increase the odds of experiencing anxiety and panic attacks simply by consuming caffeine (Nardi et al. 2009). If you struggle with anxiety of any type, you may be better off without it.

Caffeine can also induce its own anxiety and sleep disorders, and too much can lead to symptoms ranging from nervousness to tachycardia or cardiac arrhythmia (American Psychiatric Association 2000). And with its long half-life, caffeine can wreak havoc on sleep cycles, especially when consumed late in the day.

For many of my clients, simply giving up caffeine has lessened their anxiety. If you are a regular user and have any question about caffeine's effect on you, you might experiment with abstaining for two or three weeks to see if you notice any difference. See the Think Like a Shrink exercise at the end of this chapter for some guidelines on lifestyle changes.

If you decide to experiment with abstaining, be sure to check nutrition labels, because caffeine is present in a number of foods, such as sodas and chocolate. You might also taper off your consumption over the course of a few weeks (for example, cutting back by one-third for each of three weeks) in order to avoid withdrawal headaches.

ALCOHOL

Setting aside the profound problems that alcoholism can cause, even moderate use can affect our moods and our immunity against the mind.

Consider sleep, for example. Many of my clients have reported drinking a bit of alcohol to help them sleep. It usually does help—temporarily. And then it exacts a cost.

Alcohol improves sleep in nonalcoholic people for a short time, but is quickly metabolized. Within a few hours, alcohol leads to sleep disturbances, including the suppression of REM sleep, as the body adjusts to the absence of alcohol. The result? People who use alcohol to get to sleep feel sleepier the next day (Roehrs and Roth 2001).

And even moderate use of alcohol has a way of complicating problems when it is used as a solution to those problems. According to one study, for example, approximately 20 percent of people (especially men) diagnosed with post-traumatic stress disorder try to treat their symptoms using alcohol. They use it to lift their mood or to medicate symptoms away. Unfortunately, they reported worse mood and more interpersonal difficulties than people with PTSD who do not use alcohol to self-medicate (Leeies et al. 2010).

Obviously, alcohol can cause many problems, some quite severe. Using it to manage sleep, mood, and anxiety problems are just a few behaviors that can cause alcohol use to backfire. Things can get *much* worse when we use it to escape our own thoughts, feelings, and memories.

Alcohol is another substance that lends itself well to experiments in abstaining as described in the Think Like a Shrink exercise later in this chapter. In the case of alcohol, I recommend abstaining for a full month in order to understand its effects. If you have difficulty abstaining for a brief period, you will have gained valuable information. That may be an indication that it's time to enlist professional help.

In extreme cases, sudden abstinence from alcohol can cause dangerous withdrawal symptoms. If you consume large amounts, please consult with a physician about the best way to cut back on alcohol.

Exercise

It's no secret that exercise can decrease the risk of physical problems such as obesity, cardiovascular diseases, type 2 diabetes, and osteoporosis. Rod Dishman et al. (2006) also found numerous mental benefits. Regular exercise can protect against Parkinson's disease, Alzheimer's dementia, and ischemic stroke, and it helps mitigate the hormonal effects of stress.

Dishman and colleagues also found that exercise improves depression, sleep quality, and cognitive functioning. In my practice, I have noticed remarkable improvements in the mood of clients who suffer from depression and anxiety and are willing to begin an exercise regimen. Usually they report increased energy, better mood, and an improved ability to distance themselves from troubling thoughts.

It's not a miracle cure, but in my experience it is often as good as, or better than, antidepressants for clients who are willing to stick to it. A study by Mead and colleagues (2009) reported similar results. (I should also note that exercise can worsen the situation for people who find it to be a miserable or painful experience.)

In addition to the long-term, daily benefits, moderate-to-vigorous exercise can provide an immediate improvement in mood, even among people who don't regularly exercise (Maraki et al. 2005). That means that a quick trip to the gym can have an immediate effect. And unlike antidepressant medication, which can take weeks to kick in, there are no ugly side effects.

If structured exercise isn't your idea of fun, there are plenty of other options for breaking a sweat, such as dancing, martial arts, or even taking a brisk walk a few times per week. If it's been a while since you exercised, follow the old adage: start low and go slow in order to avoid a bad experience.

Sleep

I'm sure you've heard it before: Americans don't get enough sleep. Sixty percent of us sleep less than seven hours per night on average, and the same percentage have problems sleeping at least a few nights each week (Winerman 2004). That has serious implications for our ability to withstand and distance ourselves from our own minds.

Studies have found mixed effects of sleep deprivation on cognitive abilities. One study, for example, found that some aspects of cognition, such as recall and working memory, decline during sleep deprivation while other cognitive processes, like verbal fluency, might actually improve in some cases (Tucker et al. 2010).

However, the general consensus seems to be that mental functioning declines during sleep deprivation, and that the ability to sustain attention is one of the first things to go (Lim and Dinges 2010). Pilcher and Huffcutt (1996) found that sleep deprivation strongly impairs functioning, with mood being affected even more than cognitive abilities.

Sleep deprivation can lead to a less positive affect, increased anxiety, and even a bit of paranoia. Adolescent participants in one study rated the likelihood of potential catastrophes as higher when they were sleep-deprived than when they were rested (Talbot et al. 2010).

Sleep deprivation can also cause us to misread social cues. When we are sleep deprived, we can experience a blunted recognition of moderately happy and angry facial expressions, though we seem to have no difficulty recognizing sad expressions (van der Helm, Gujar, and Walker 2010). Add that to the perceptual changes of low mood, and you have a mind that may be giving you very inaccurate information about the world.

Like exercise and diet, your sleep schedule should be tailored to you, and you probably already have a good idea of what works best. If you want to increase your immunity against the thoughts and feelings your mind throws at you, consider these questions: How many hours of sleep do you need before you awaken naturally, feeling refreshed? What is the best time for you to sleep—are you naturally a morning person or an evening person? Do naps help or hinder your sleep cycle?

Where pharmacological sleep aids are concerned, it's best to consult with a physician who is familiar with you. They can be useful tools for getting your sleep back on track, but they're generally not a good long-term solution. If you simply cannot get good sleep no matter what you try, you should probably visit a sleep clinic to diagnose the problem.

Like a sleep-deprived child, a sleep-deprived mind is irritable, irrational, and difficult to live with. It throws off our perceptions and our abilities.

By now, you may be wondering if it would be useful to make some changes in your diet, exercise, or sleep habits. Change is rarely easy, and so it helps to know if the benefit of a change will outweigh the effort involved. This next exercise will help you approach change the way a psychologist might: methodically and in small steps.

Exercise: Think Like a Shrink

This exercise requires a commitment of up to six weeks,* but it can yield a rich payoff. It's designed to help you discover what kind of changes best benefit you in the realm of diet, exercise, sleep, or any other lifestyle category you might be contemplating. You may wish to consult with a medical professional before making radical changes, and I don't say that merely as a legal formality. Many mistakes can be made in matters like diet and exercise, and there are helpful ways to ease the transition into new habits. We want your efforts to result in positive lifestyle changes rather than discouragement. For that same reason, it's important to start small. The goal is to experiment with small behavior changes in order to see if they're beneficial. If so, they can be expanded upon. There are five steps involved. They require a bit of diligence but very little time.

1. Choose an area of focus—diet, exercise, sleep, or some other lifestyle change that's important to you. Identify some small change you would like to experiment with, such as abstaining from caffeine or going for a walk each morning.

2. For the first three weeks, continue your habits without change while monitoring your energy level, mood, and ability to distance yourself from thoughts and feelings—let's call that last one "presence," as in staying present in the moment and observing the mind from a distance. You may choose to monitor other variables as well—such as your blood pressure or the quality of your sleep. At regular intervals each day (for example, 10 a.m., 3 p.m., and 8 p.m.) rate your variables using a ten-point rating scale: 1 = the worst and 10 = the best. Record any other pertinent observations (e.g., good day at work, argument with spouse, and so on). We'll call these first three weeks your "baseline"—a record of your usual behavior. You can use a copy of the worksheet below to record your ratings.

You can adjust the time period as appropriate for your situation. For example, you may require only a week or two to become familiar with your baseline, but I recommend instituting your chosen lifestyle change for at least three weeks. That should be enough time for you to adjust to the change (working through caffeine withdrawal, for example), with time left over to develop a clear understanding of the effect. Three weeks is also long enough to give you a good start on your habit should you choose to keep it. If you feel ambivalent about keeping the new habit, you can always return to your baseline behavior for a while to see what changes you notice.

Baseline Behavior Record

Week number: _____

Tracked behavior: _____

_____

_____

	Energy	Mood	Presence	Other	Observations
Sunday					
10:00 a.m.					
3:00 p.m.					
8:00 p.m.					
Monday					
10:00 a.m.					
3:00 p.m.					
8:00 p.m.					
Tuesday					
10:00 a.m.					
3:00 p.m.					
8:00 p.m.					

Wednesday					
10:00 a.m.					
3:00 p.m.					
8:00 p.m.					
Thursday					
10:00 a.m.					
3:00 p.m.					
8:00 p.m.					
Friday					
10:00 a.m.					
3:00 p.m.					
8:00 p.m.					
Saturday					
10:00 a.m.					
3:00 p.m.					
8:00 p.m.					

1 = Worst; 10 = Best

3. After the first three weeks, institute the behavioral change. Write the change you've chosen to make on a copy of the worksheet below. For example, "Decrease caffeine use by 2 cups a day," "Walk fifteen minutes each day," or "Go to bed by 10 p.m." Remember, start with a small, specific change. Overly ambitious goals increase the risk of failure.

4. For the next three weeks, incorporate the change you've chosen into your daily life. Again, monitor your energy level, mood, and ability to distance yourself from thoughts and feelings ("presence") at regular intervals each day, using the ten-point rating scale (0 = the worst, 10 = the best). Record any other pertinent observations.

Changed Behavior Record

Week number: _____

Tracked behavior: _____

_____

_____

	Energy	Mood	Presence	Other	Observations
Sunday					
10:00 a.m.					
3:00 p.m.					
8:00 p.m.					
Monday					
10:00 a.m.					
3:00 p.m.					
8:00 p.m.					
Tuesday					
10:00 a.m.					
3:00 p.m.					
8:00 p.m.					
Wednesday					
10:00 a.m.					
3:00 p.m.					
8:00 p.m.					

Thursday					
10:00 a.m.					
3:00 p.m.					
8:00 p.m.					
Friday					
10:00 a.m.					
3:00 p.m.					
8:00 p.m.					
Saturday					
10:00 a.m.					
3:00 p.m.					
8:00 p.m.					

1 = Worst; 10 = Best

5. At the end of the second three weeks, you can compare the two time periods and evaluate the usefulness of the change. You might take averages of the ratings you recorded. How did your energy level, mood, and presence change over the second three-week period? Will it be worthwhile to maintain the new habit?

Lifestyle choices can have a profound effect on our moods and mental states. That, in turn, can affect the ability to distance ourselves from our own minds. A good physical state makes it that much easier to gain distance from thoughts and feelings and to drop the battle against our own minds.

One Final Exercise: Increasing Psychological Flexibility for a Lifetime

I encourage you to try one more exercise. It is probably the most difficult exercise of the book, and it can yield the greatest benefit. It is simply this: identify that which you fear, and move toward it.

I'm not suggesting that you should belly flop into a pool of alligators simply because it frightens you. Many things in the world *should* be feared, and perhaps that's why the mind excels at that particular emotion.

Nor am I suggesting that you should do random, frightening things like performing a sexy striptease at the local food court. I've never advocated discomfort (or getting arrested) merely for the sake of it.

I am talking about a fear-provoking activity that is much more substantive: moving in the direction of your values.

I knew a man who earned a very comfortable living in a job that meant very little to him. Every day he was unhappy because there was another profession that suited his values but offered much less pay. For years, he struggled with the possibility of changing careers but could not bring himself to give up his salary and security.

It was only when he became utterly miserable that he realized he had no choice. He resigned his position and embarked on his new career as a pastor. Even though life was difficult for a time and he had to give up a great many things to pursue the necessary education, he experienced a joy he had never imagined. It was the joy that comes from living in accordance with one's values. He discovered that the austerity of his new life was a small price to pay.

Living up to one's values rarely requires such drastic measures. More often, our values demand smaller changes. Even so, moving in the direction of our values is often difficult. By their very nature, the actions most consistent with our values also hold our greatest vulnerabilities. The person who seeks love must risk heartbreak. It hurts to fail at something we care about.

Yet a strange thing happens when we embrace fear and pursue what matters to us: our horizons expand in all directions. The fear that keeps us from our values is like a chain around our neck, anchored firmly to a safe spot on the ground. When we add new behaviors to our repertoire—especially behaviors consistent with our values—that chain is weakened and we are free to move farther in all directions. With values-consistent action, our entire world expands.

How to Disobey a Human Mind

Expanding our world often means disobeying the mind, and disobeying the mind gets easier with practice. Each time we choose our own path rather than following the protective dictates of the mind, our world grows a bit in all directions, our options flourish, and we reassert our claim to freedom. Disobeying the mind begins with a few basic practices:

Observation. Learning to watch the mind is a significant challenge—not because doing so is inherently difficult, but because it is so darned easy to forget. We are immersed in a world of thoughts, feelings, and words. Observing the mind is a skill that simply takes diligent practice to develop. (See chapter 3.)

Insight. Choosing whether or not to obey the mind is easier when we know what the mind trying to accomplish. All minds share some things in common, such as an overriding concern for survival. Each mind also has its own unique learning history that it uses to guide us—or imprison us, as the case may be. Understanding the effects of history—to know thyself, as the ancient Greek adage goes—requires special effort, which can be aided by a skilled psychologist. (See chapters 4 and 5.)

Values-driven action. Minds can befuddle us with exceedingly persuasive thoughts and feelings. Clearly defined values give us a reference point outside our own thoughts and feelings. They serve as a guide when we are lost in a morass of our own internal experiences. Values help us fight for what we want rather than fighting an endless battle against that which we don't want. (See chapter 6.)

Some of the strategies we've discussed are better suited for calm moments, such as defining values and building the skills of observation. Others are useful in crisis situations when the mind has us cornered. Those include techniques such as doing the opposite of what the mind says, recognizing and responding to the mind's trump cards, and steadying ourselves on the knowledge that the mind might possibly be wrong.

One skill that applies across circumstances is gratitude for the mind. No matter how anxious or sullen they may be, our minds are always looking out for us. If you'll indulge me in one last sentiment, let's pay homage to these worry machines of ours:

> *Thank you, mind, for keeping me alive. Thank you for protecting me from speeding buses, bad guys, and angry bosses. Thank you for your paranoia, worry, and angst. I know you think it's effective, and maybe you're right sometimes. Thank you for saving me from* [fill in your own harrowing experiences] *and for your endless reminders to prevent them from happening again. Thank you for always keeping me company. Even though you annoy the heck out of me sometimes, you often stumble onto good ideas. And though I won't always obey you from now on, I promise to be respectful of your intentions and grateful for your ever-watchful eye.*

When your mind is doing its worst, take comfort in the knowledge that it will not last. There will always be one more memory, one more feeling, and one more state of mind. Minds never stop talking, and they rarely speak plainly. They can be unruly, intrusive, and downright painful to live with.

They are also our best friends and the first things keeping us safe in a danger-ous world.

The mind can be trained, but its nature cannot be changed. Living peaceably with this cantankerous bundle of neurons requires the skill to deci-pher its messages, the willingness to accept all that it gives, and the fortitude to make choices that cause it to protest. I wish you well as you enjoy the free-dom brought by peaceful coexistence with your own human mind.

References

American Psychiatric Association. 2000. *Diagnostic and Statistical Manual of Mental Disorders*. 4th ed., text revision. Washington, DC: American Psychiatric Association.

Andrews, P. W., and J. A. Thomson Jr. 2009. "The Bright Side of Being Blue: Depression as an Adaptation for Analyzing Complex Problems." *Psychological Review* 116: 620–54.

Avramova, Y. R., D. A. Stapel, and D. Lerouge. 2010. "Mood and Context-Dependence: Positive Mood Increases and Negative Mood Decreases the Effects of Context on Perception." *Journal of Personality and Social Psychology* 99: 203–14.

Bach, P. A., B. Gaudiano, J. Pankey, J. D. Herbert, and S. C. Hayes. 2006. "Acceptance, Mindfulness, Values, and Psychosis: Applying Acceptance and Commitment Therapy (ACT) to the Chronically Mentally Ill." In *Mindfulness-Based Treatment Approaches: Clinician's Guide to Evidence Base and Application*, edited by R. A. Baer. Burlington, MA: Elsevier.

Baer, R. A. 2010. "Mindfulness- and Acceptance-Based Interventions and Processes of Change." In *Assessing Mindfulness and Acceptance Processes in Clients: Illuminating the Theory and Practice of Change*, edited by R. A. Baer. Oakland, CA: New Harbinger Publications.

Barnes, R. D., and S. Tantleff-Dunn. 2010. "Food for Thought: Examining the Relationship Between Food Thought Suppression and Weight-Related Outcomes."1 *Eating Behaviors* 11: 175–79.

Barnes-Holmes, D., S. C. Hayes, and S. Dymond. 2001. "Self and Self-Directed Rules." In *Relational Frame Theory: A Post-Skinnerian Account of Human Language and Cognition*, edited by Steven C. Hayes, Dermot Barnes-Holmes, and Bryan Roche. New York: Kluwer Academic/Plenum Publishers.

Barrett, H. C. 2005. "Adaptations to Predators and Prey." In *The Handbook of Evolutionary Psychology*, edited by David M. Buss. Hoboken, NJ: John Wiley & Sons.

Benton, D. 2002. "Carbohydrate Ingestion, Blood Glucose, and Mood." *Neuroscience and Biobehavioral Reviews* 26: 293–308.

Blaney, P. H. 1986. "Affect and Memory: A Review." *Psychological Bulletin* 99: 229–46.

Block, J. A., and E. Wulfert. 2000. "Acceptance or Change: Treating Socially Anxious College Students with ACT or CBGT." *The Behavior Analyst Today* 1: 2–10.

Bower, G. H. 1981. "Mood and Memory." *American Psychologist* 36: 129–48.

Bretherton, I., and K. A. Munholland. 1999. "Internal Working Models in Attachment Relationships: A Construct Revisited." In *Handbook of Attachment: Theory, Research, and Clinical Applications*, edited by Jude Cassidy and Phillip R. Shaver. New York: Guilford Press.

Brüne, M. 2006. "The Evolutionary Psychology of Obsessive-Compulsive Disorder: The Role of Cognitive Metarepresentation." *Perspectives in Biology and Medicine* 49: 317–29.

Cantor, C. 2005. *Evolution and Posttraumatic Stress: Disorders of Vigilance and Defence.* New York: Routledge.

Cascade, E. F., A. H. Kalali, and P. Blier. 2007. "Treatment of Depression: Antidepressant Monotherapy and Combination Therapy." *Psychiatry* 4: 25–27.

Corsica, J. A., and B. J. Spring. 2008. "Carbohydrate Craving: A Double-Blind, Placebo-Controlled Test of the Self-Medication Hypothesis." *Eating Behaviors* 9: 447–54.

Dahl, J. C., J. C. Plumb, I. Steward, and T. Lundren. 2009. *The Art and Science of Valuing in Psychotherapy.* Oakland, CA: New Harbinger Publications.

Dalgleish, T., J. Yiend, S. Schweizer, and B. D. Dunn. 2009. "Ironic Effects of Emotion Suppression When Recounting Distressing Memories." *Emotion* 9: 744–49.

del Valle, C. H. C., and P. M. Mateos. 2008. "Dispositional Pessimism, Defensive Pessimism, and Optimism: The Effect of Induced Mood on Prefactual and Counterfactual Thinking and Performance." *Cognition & Emotion* 22: 1600–12.

De Martino, B., C. F. Camerer, and R. Adolphs. 2010. "Amygdala Damage Eliminated Monetary Loss Aversion." *Proceedings of the National Academy of Sciences of the United States of America* 107: 3788–92.

Dishman, R. K., H.-R. Berthoud, F. W. Booth, C. W. Cotman, V. R. Edgerton, M. R. Fleshner, S. C. Gandevia, F. Gomez-Pinilla, B. N. Greenwood, C. H. Hillman, A. F. Kramer, B. E. Levin, T. H. Moran, A. A. Russo-Neustadt, J. D. Salamone, J. D. Van

Hoomissen, C. E. Wade, D. A. York, and M. J. Zigmond. 2006. "Neurobiology of Exercise." *Obesity* 14: 345–56.

Dobson, K. S., S. D. Hollon, S. Dimidjian, K. B. Schmaling, R. J. Kohlenberg, R. J. Gallop, S. L. Rizvi, J. K. Gollan, D. L. Dunner, and N. S. Jacobson. 2008. "Randomized Trial of Behavioral Activation, Cognitive Therapy, and Antidepressant Medication in the Prevention of Relapse and Recurrence in Major Depression." *Journal of Consulting and Clinical Psychology* 76: 468–77.

Dryden, W., and A. Ellis. 2001. "Rational Emotive Behavior Therapy." In *Handbook of Cognitive Behavioral Therapies. 2nd ed.*, edited by Keith S. Dobson. New York: Guilford Press.

Duntley, J. D. 2005. "Adaptations to Dangers from Humans." In *The Handbook of Evolutionary Psychology*, edited by David M. Buss. Hoboken, NJ: John Wiley & Sons.

Eisenberger, N. I., and M. D. Lieberman. 2004. "Why Rejection Hurts: A Common Neural Alarm System for Physical and Social Pain." *TRENDS in Cognitive Sciences* 8: 294–300.

Ellis, H. C., R. L. Thomas, A. D. McFarland, and W. Lane. 1985. "Emotional Mood States and Retrieval in Episodic Memory." *Journal of Experimental Psychology* 11: 363–70.

Esquivel, G., K. R. Schruers, R. J. Maddock, A. Colasanti, and E. J. Griez. 2010. "Acids in the Brain: A Factor in Panic?" *Journal of Psychopharmacology* 24: 639–47.

Festinger, L. 1954. "A Theory of Social Comparison Process." *Human Relations* 7: 117–40.

Fields, C. 2002. "Why Do We Talk to Ourselves?" *Journal of Experimental & Theoretical Artificial Intelligence* 14: 255–72.

Forgas, J. P. 2007. "When Sad Is Better than Happy: Negative Affect Can Improve the Quality and Effectiveness of Persuasive Messages and Social Influence Strategies." *Journal of Experimental Social Psychology* 43: 513–28.

Forgas, J. P., L. Goldenberg, and C. Unkelbach. 2009. "Can Bad Weather Improve Your Memory? An Unobtrusive Field Study of Natural Mood Effects on Real-Life Memory." *Journal of Experimental Social Psychology* 45: 254–57.

Frankland, P. W., B. Bontempi, L. E. Talton, L. Kaczmarek, and A. Silva. 2004. "The Involvement of the Anterior Cingulate Cortex in Remote Contextual Fear Memory." *Science* 304: 881–83.

Garcia, J., W. G. Hankins, and K. W. Rusniak. 1976. "Flavor Aversion Studies." *Science* 192: 265–66.

Gasper, K., R. H. Lozinski, and L. S. LeBeau. 2009. "If You Plan, Then You Can: How Reflection Helps Defensive Pessimists Pursue Their Goals." *Motivation and Emotion* 33: 203–16.

Gordon, R. A. 2008. "Attributional Style and Athletic Performance: Strategic Optimism and Defensive Pessimism." *Psychology of Sport and Exercise* 9: 336–50.

Haselton, M. G., D. Nettle, and P. W. Andrews. 2005. "The Evolution of Cognitive Bias." In *The Handbook of Evolutionary Psychology*, edited by David M. Buss. Hoboken, NJ: John Wiley & Sons.

Hayes, S. C., K. D. Strosahl, and K. G. Wilson. 1999. *Acceptance and Commitment Therapy: An Experiential Approach to Behavior Change*. New York: Guilford Press.

Hinton, D., and S. Hinton. 2002. "Panic Disorder, Somatization, and the New Cross-Cultural Psychiatry: The Seven Bodies of a Medical Anthropology of Panic." *Culture, Medicine, and Psychiatry* 26: 155–78

Hoffman, S. G., and D. A. Moscovitch. 2002. "Evolutionary Mechanisms of Fear and Anxiety." *Journal of Cognitive Psychotherapy* 16: 317–30.

Hooker, C. I., S. C. Verosky, L. T. Germine, R. T. Knight, and M. D'Esposito. 2010. "Neural Activity During Social Signal Perception Correlates with Self-Reported Empathy." *Brain Research* 1308: 100–13.

Hosogoshi, H., and M. Kodama. 2009. "Accepting Pessimistic Thinking Is Associated with Better Mental and Physical Health in Defensive Pessimists." *Japanese Journal of Psychology* 79: 542–48.

Howard, G. S., M. Y. Lau, S. E. Maxwell, A. Venter, R. Lundy, and R. M. Sweeny. 2009. "Do Research Literatures Give Correct Answers?" *Review of General Psychology* 13: 116–21.

Ivy, J. L, D. L. Costill, W. J. Fink, and R. W. Lower. 1979. "Influence of Caffeine and Carbohydrate Feedings on Endurance Performance." *Medicine & Science in Sports & Exercise* 11: 6–11.

Jacka, F. N., J. A. Pasco, A. Mykletun, L. J. Williams, A. M. Hodge, S. L. O'Reilly, G. C. Nicholson, M. A. Kotowicz, and M. Berk. 2010. "Association of Western and Traditional Diets with Depression and Anxiety in Women." *American Journal of Psychiatry* 167: 305–11.

James, W. 1892. *Psychology*. New York: World.

Jelinek, L., C. Stockbauer, S. Randjbar, M. Kellner, T. Ehring, and S. Moritz. 2010. "Characteristics and Organization of the Worst Moment of Trauma Memories in Posttraumatic Stress Disorder." *Behaviour Research and Therapy* 48: 680–85.

Jureidini, J., and A. Tonkin. 2006. "Overuse of Antidepressant Drugs for the Treatment of Depression." *CNS Drugs* 20: 623–32.

Kanter, J. W., A. M. Busch, and L. C. Rusch. 2009. *Behavioral Activation*. New York: Routledge.

Keeley, J., R. Zayac, and C. Correia. 2008. "Curvilinear Relationships Between Statistics Anxiety and Performance Among Undergraduate Students: Evidence for Optimal Anxiety." *Statistics Education Research Journal* 7: 4–15.

Kenealy, P. M. 1997. "Mood-State-Dependent Retrieval: The Effects of Induced Mood on Memory Reconsidered." *Quarterly Journal of Experimental Psychology* 50A: 290–317.

Kessler, R. C., W. T. Chiu, O. Demler, and E. E. Waters. 2005. "Prevalence, Severity, and Comorbidity of 12-Month DSM-IV Disorders in the National Comorbidity Survey Replication." *Archives of General Psychiatry* 62: 617–27.

Kircher, T. T. J., and D. T. Leube. 2003. "Self-Consciousness, Self-Agency, and Schizophrenia." *Consciousness and Cognition* 12: 656–69.

Klüver, H., and P. C. Bucy. 1939. "Preliminary Analysis of Functions of the Temporal Lobes in Monkeys." *Archives of Neurology and Psychiatry* 42: 979–1000.

Kosslyn, S. M., W. L. Thompson, I. J. Kim, and N. M. Alpert. 1995. "Topographical Representations of Mental Images in Primary Visual Cortex." *Nature* 378: 496–98.

Kremkow, J., A. Aertsen, and A. Kumar. 2010. "Gating of Signal Propagation in Spiking Neural Networks by Balanced and Correlated Excitation and Inhibition." *Journal of Neuroscience* 30: 15760–68.

Lavy, E. H., and M. A. Van den Hout. 1990. "Thought Suppression Induces Intrusion." *Behavioural and Cognitive Psychotherapy* 18: 251–58.

Leahy, R. L. 2002. "Pessimism and the Evolution of Negativity." *Journal of Cognitive Psychotherapy: An International Quarterly* 16: 295–316.

Leeies, M., J. Pagura, J. Sareen, and J. M. Bolton. 2010. "The Use of Alcohol and Drugs to Self-Medicate Symptoms of Posttraumatic Stress Disorder." *Depression and Anxiety* 27: 731–36.

Lehrer, J. 2009. "Don't! The Secret of Self-Control." *The New Yorker*, May 18, 26[SSI].

Lieberman, M. D. 2000. "Intuition: A Social Cognitive Neuroscience Approach." *Psychological Bulletin* 126: 109–37.

Lim, L. 2009. "A Two-Factor Model of Defensive Pessimism and Its Relations with Achievement Motives." *The Journal of Psychology* 143: 318–36.

Lim, J., and D. F. Dinges. 2010. "A Meta-analysis of the Impact of Short-Term Sleep Deprivation on Cognitive Variables." *Psychological Bulletin* 136: 375–89.

Lin, L., R. Osan, and J. Z. Tsien. 2006. "Organizing Principles of Real-Time Memory Encoding: Neural Clique Assemblies and Universal Neural Codes. *Trends in Neuroscience* 29: 48–57.

Linden, D..E. J. 2006. "How Psychotherapy Changes the Brain: The Contribution of Functional Neuroimaging." *Molecular Psychiatry* 11: 528–38.

Linehan, M. M. 1993. *Skills Training Manual for Treating Borderline Personality Disorder.* New York: Guilford Press.

Liu, X.-H., S.-Q. Yao, W.-F. Zhao, W.-H. Yang, and F.-R. Tan. 2010. "Autobiographical Memory in Patients with Chronic Pain and Depression." *Chinese Journal of Clinical Psychology* 18: 196–201.

LoBue, V. 2010. "And Along Came a Spider: An Attentional Bias for the Detection of Spiders in Young Children and Adults." *Journal of Experimental Child Psychology* 107: 59–66.

Lou, H. C., J. Gross, K. Biermann-Ruben, T. W. Kjaer, and A. Schnitzler. "Coherence in Consciousness: Paralimbic Gamma Synchrony of Self-Reference Links Conscious Experiences." *Human Brain Mapping* 31: 185–92.

Lyubomirsky, S., L. Sousa, and R. Dickerhoof. 2006. "The Costs and Benefits of Writing, Talking, and Thinking About Life's Triumphs and Defeats." *Journal of Personality and Social Psychology* 90: 692–708.

MacLean, P. D. 1973. *A Triune Concept of the Brain and Behavior.* Toronto: University of Toronto Press.

Maraki, M., F. Tsoflioua, Y. P. Pitsiladisb, D. Malkovaa, N. Mutriea, and S. Higgins. 2005. "Acute Effects of a Single Exercise Class on Appetite, Energy Intake, and Mood: Is There a Time of Day Effect?" *Appetite* 45: 272–78.

Marian, V., and M. Kaushanskaya. 2007. "Language Context Guides Memory Content." *Psychonomic Bulletin & Review* 14: 925–33.

Martell, C. R., S. Dimidjian, and R. Herman-Dunn. 2010. *Behavioral Activation for Depression: A Clinician's Guide.* New York: Guilford Press.

Mathews, R. C., L. G. Roussel, B. P. Cochran, A. E. Cook, and D. L. Dunaway. 2000. "The Role of Implicit Learning in the Acquisition of Generative Knowledge." *Journal of Cognitive Systems Research* 1: 161–74.

Mead, G. E., W. Morley, P. Campbell, C. A. Greig, M. E. T. McMurdo, and D. A. Lawlor. 2009. "Exercise for Depression." *Mental Health and Physical Activity* 2: 95–96.

Mischel, W., Y. Shoda, and M. L. Rodriguez. 1989. "Delay of Gratification in Children." *Science* 244: 933–38.

Nardi, A. E., F. L. Lopes, R. C. Freire, A. B. Veras, I. Nascimento, A. M. Valenca, V. L. de-Melo-Neto, G. L. Soares-Filho, A. L. King, D. M. Arau´jo, M. A. Mezzasalma, A. Rassi, W. A. Zin. 2009. "Panic Disorder and Social Anxiety Disorder Subtypes in a Caffeine Challenge Test. *Psychiatry Research* 169: 149–53.

Nelson, E. A., B. J. Deacon, J. J. Lickel, and J. T. Sy. 2010. "Targeting the Probability Versus Cost of Feared Outcomes in Public Speaking Anxiety." *Behaviour Research and Therapy* 48: 282–89.

Norem, J. K. 2008. "Defensive Pessimism, Anxiety, and the Complexity of Evaluating Self-Regulation." *Social and Personality Psychology Compass* 2: 121–34.

Orsillo, S. M., L. Roemer, J. Block-Lerner, C. LeJeune, and J. D. Herbert. 2004. "ACT with Anxiety Disorders." In *A Practical Guide to Acceptance and Commitment Therapy*, edited by Steven C. Hayes and Kirk D. Strosahl. New York: Springer.

Ostroff, L. E., C. K. Cain, J. Bedont, M. H. Monfils, and J. E. LeDoux. 2010. "Fear and Safety Learning Differentially Affect Synapse Size and Dendritic Translation in the Lateral Amygdala." *Proceedings of the National Academy of Sciences* 107: 9418–423.

Pilcher, J. J., and A. I. Huffcutt. 1996. "Effects of Sleep Deprivation on Performance: A Meta-analysis." *Sleep* 19: 318–26.

Pinker, S. 2007. *How the Mind Works*. New York: W. W. Norton & Company.

Poulos, A. M., V. Li, S. S. Sterlace, F. Tokushige, R. Ponnusamy, and M. S. Fanselow. "Persistence of Fear Memory Across Time Requires the Basolateral Amygdala Complex." *Proceedings of the National Academy of Sciences* 106: 11737–41.

Purdon, C., K. Rowa, and M. M. Antony. 2005. "Thought Suppression and Its Effects on Thought Frequency, Appraisal, and Mood State in Individuals with Obsessive-Compulsive Disorder." *Behaviour Research and Therapy* 43: 93–108.

Quinn, J. M., A. Pascoe, W. Wood, and D. T. Neal. 2010. "Can't Control Yourself? Monitor Those Bad Habits." *Personality and Social Psychology Bulletin* 36: 499–511.

Raglin, J. S., and P. E. Turner. 1993. "Anxiety and Performance in Track and Field Athletes: A Comparison of the Inverted-U Hypothesis with Zone of Optimal Function Theory." *Personality and Individual Differences* 14: 163–71.

Ramnerö, J., and N. Törneke. 2008. *The ABCs of Human Behavior*. Oakland, CA: New Harbinger.

Rassin, E. 2005. *Thought Supression*. Oxford, UK: Elsevier.

Rizvi, S. L., and M. M. Linehan. 2005. "Treatment of Maladaptive Shame in Borderline Personality Disorder: A Pilot Study of 'Opposite Action.'" *Cognitive and Behavioral Practice* 12: 437–47.

Roehrs, T., and T. Roth. 2001. "Sleep, Sleepiness, and Alcohol Use." *Alcohol Research and Health* 25: 101–9.

Rysen, S. 2006. "Publication of Nonsignificant Results: A Survey of Psychologists' Opinions." *Psychological Reports* 98: 169–75.

Sadock, B. J., and V. A. Sadock. 2003. *Synopsis of Psychiatry: Behavioral Sciences/Clinical Psychiatry*. Philadelphia: Lippencott Williams & Wilkins.

Schlund, M. W., G. J. Siegle, C. D. Ladouceur, J. S. Silk, M. F. Cataldo, E. E. Forbes, R. E. Dahl, and N. D. Ryan. 2010. "Nothing to Fear? Neural Systems Supporting Avoidance Behavior in Healthy Youths." *NeuroImage* 52: 710–19.

Schmid, P. C., and M. S. Mast. 2010. "Mood Effects on Emotion Regulation." *Motivation and Emotion* 34: 288–92.

Seery, M. D., T. V. West, M. Weisbuch, and J. Blascovich. 2008. "The Effects of Negative Reflection for Defensive Pessimists: Dissipation or Harnessing of Threat?" *Personality and Individual Differences* 45: 515–20.

Seger, C. A. 1994. "Implicit Learning." *Psychological Bulletin* 115: 163–96.

Seligman, M. P. 2006. *Learned Optimism: How to Change Your Mind and Your Life*. New York: Vintage Books.

Shallcross, A. J., A. S. Troy, M. Boland, and I. B. Iris. 2010. "Let It Be: Accepting Negative Emotional Experiences Predicts Decreased Negative Affect and Depressive Symptoms." *Behaviour Research and Therapy* 48: 921–29.

Sidman, M. 1953. "Avoidance Conditioning with Brief Shock and No Exteroceptive Warning Signal." *Science* 118: 157–58.

Smith, S. T. "Preventing Violence Among Patients Recovering from Traumatic Brain Injury: A Response Curriculum for Medical and Support Staff." Diss. University of Denver, 2006. Print.

Snyder, H. R., N. Hutchison, E. Nyhus, T. Curran, M. T. Banich, R. C. O'Reilly, and Y. Munakata. 2010. "Neural Inhibition Enables Selection During Language Processing." *Proceedings of the National Academy of Sciences* 107: 16483–88.

Tai, S., and D. Turkington. 2009. "The Evolution of Cognitive Behavior Therapy for Schizophrenia: Current Practice and Recent Developments." *Schizophrenia Bulletin* 35: 865–73.

Talbot, L. S., E. L. McGlinchey, K. A. Kaplan, R. E. Dahl, and A. G. Harvey. 2010. "Sleep Deprivation in Adolescents and Adults: Changes in Affect. *Emotion* 10: 831–41.

Tucker, A. M., P. Whitney, G. Belenky, J. M. Hinson, and H. P. A. Van Dongen. 2010. "Effects of Sleep Deprivation on Dissociated Components of Executive Functioning. *Sleep* 33: 47–57.

Van Bockstaele, B., B. Verschuere, J. De Houwer, and G. Crombez. 2010. "On the Costs and Benefits of Directing Attention Towards or Away from Threat-Related Stimuli: A Classical Conditioning Experiment." *Behaviour Research and Therapy* 48: 692–97.

van der Helm, E., N. Gujar, and M. P. Walker. 2010. "Sleep Deprivation Impairs the Accurate Recognition of Human Emotions. *Sleep* 33: 335–42.

Vogels, T. P., and L. F. Abbot. 2009. "Gating Multiple Signals Through Detailed Balance of Excitation and Inhibition in Spiking Networks." *Nature Neuroscience* 12: 483–91.

Wagar, B. M., and P. Thagard. 2004. "Spiking Phineas Gage: A Neurocomputational Theory of Cognitive-Affective Integration in Decision Making." *Psychological Review* 111: 67–79.

Watkins, P. C., K. Vache, S. P. Verney, S. Muller, and A. Matthews. 1996. "Unconscious Mood-Congruent Memory Bias in Depression. *Journal of Abnormal Psychology* 105: 34–41.

Wegner, D. M., D. J. Schneider, S. R. Carter, and T. L. White. 1987. "Paradoxical Effects of Thought Suppression." *Journal of Personality and Social Psychology* 53: 5–13.

Westover, A. N., and L. B. Marangell. 2002. "A Cross-national Relationship Between Sugar Consumption and Major Depression? *Depression and Anxiety* 16: 118–20.

Wilson, K. G., and T. Dufrene. 2008. *Mindfulness for Two: An Acceptance and Commitment Therapy Approach to Mindfulness in Psychotherapy.* Oakland, CA: New Harbinger.

Wilson, K. G., S. C. Hayes, J. Gregg, and R. Zettle. 2001. "Psychopathology and Psychotherapy." In *Relational Frame Theory: A Post-Skinnerian Account of Human Language and Cognition*, edited by Steven C. Hayes, Dermot Barnes-Holms, and Bryan Roche. New York: Kluwer Academic/Plenum Publishers.

Wilson, K. G., E. K. Sandoz, J. Kitchens, and M. Roberts. 2010. "The Valued Living Questionnaire: Defining and Measuring Valued Action Within a Behavioral Framework." *The Psychological Record* 60: 249–72.

Winerman, L. 2004. "Sleep Deprivation Threatens Public Health, Says Research Award Winner." *Monitor on Psychology* 35: 61.

Wood, R. Ll. 2001. "Understanding Neurobehavioural Disability." In *Neurobehavioural Disability and Social Handicap Following Traumatic Brain Injury*, edited by Rodger Ll. Wood and Tom M. McMillan. East Sussex, UK: Psychology Press.

Yerkes, R. M., and J. D. Dodson. 1908. "The Relation of Strength of Stimulus to Rapidity of Habit-Formation." *Journal of Comparative Neurology and Psychology* 18: 459–82.

Ziegler, R. 2010. "Mood, Source Characteristics, and Message Processing: A Mood-Congruent Expectancies Approach." *Journal of Experimental Social Psychology* 46: 743–52.

Shawn T. Smith, PsyD, is a psychologist in private practice who has enjoyed a lifelong fascination with the mind. He has done clinical work in diverse locations, including a rape crisis clinic, the International Commission on Missing Persons in Bosnia, and the Colorado prison system. Smith lives in Denver, CO, with his wife, daughter, and their dog.

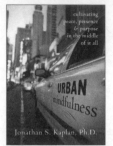